# The Great American Pop Culture Quiz Book

The editors of > **Entertainment** WEEKLY ™

POCKET BOOKS

New York | London | Toronto | Sydney

POCKET BOOKS

POCKET BOOKS, a division of Simon & Schuster, Inc.
1230 Avenue of the Americas, New York, NY 10020

Copyright © 2005 by Entertainment Weekly Inc.

© 2005 Entertainment Weekly Inc. ENTERTAINMENT WEEKLY® and ENTERTAINMENT
WEEKLY GREAT AMERICAN POP CULTURE QUIZ are trademarks of Entertainment
Weekly Inc.

ISBN-13: 978-1-4165-1057-4
ISBN-10: 1-4165-1057-5

This Pocket Books trade paperback edition September 2005

10 9 8 7 6 5 4 3 2 1

POCKET and colophon are registered trademarks of
Simon & Schuster, Inc.

Manufactured in the United States of America

For information regarding special discounts for bulk purchases, please contact
Simon & Schuster Special Sales at 1-800-456-6798 or business@simonandschuster.com

# The
# Great
# American
# Pop > **Entertainment**

The editors of

WEEKLY

TM

# Culture
# Quiz
# Book

# Contents

# 1990s

Friends, Up Close & Personal, The Wonder Years, The Truman Show, Leonardo DiCaprio, Single White Female, The Usual Suspects, Home Improvement, A League of Their Own, LeAnn Rimes, Apollo 13, NYPD Blue, The Bodyguard, Nirvana, Misery, Twister, Public Enemy, Tin Cup, L.A. Confidential, Melrose Place, Jay Leno, Gloria Estefan, Drew Carey, R.E.M., Frasier, Eyes Wide Shut, Fargo... **113**

# 2000s

The Lord of the Rings, Anchorman, Mulholland Dr., Ocean's Eleven, The West Wing, Spider-Man, Good Charlotte, My Big Fat Greek Wedding, Lost in Translation, Shallow Hal, Norah Jones, Lost, Alias, Everwood, Eternal Sunshine of the Spotless Mind, The Killers, Scrubs, Miracle, 'N Sync, Shadow of the Vampire, Million Dollar Baby, Master and Commander, CSI, Revenge of the Sith, Survivor... **149**

Thank you...

Paul Bodley, Gerry Burke, Evan Campisi, Bob Cannon, Alexander Chow, Sandy Drayton, Kristina Feliciano, Theresa Griggs, Cindy Grisolia, Jennifer Heddle, Geraldine Hessler, Paul Katz, Jeff Labrecque, Audrey Landreth, Allyssa Lee, Peggy Mansfield, Carol Mazzarella, Fiona McDonagh, Joseph McGovern, Fred Nelson, Nancy Ryan, Andy Sareyan, Amy Steiner, Claire Strupp, Rick Tetzeli, Lou Vogel, and Heidi Weinkam

# The

American art

# Culture Quiz

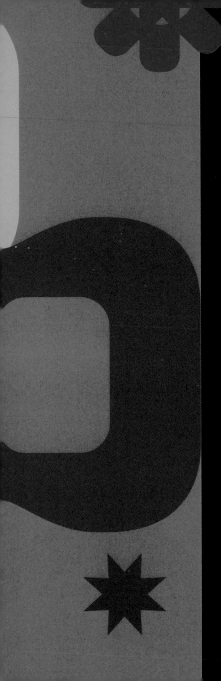

In what **movie** did Steve Guttenberg's character subject his fiancée to a **quiz** on football? Barry Levinson's 1982 comedy, *Diner*. If she passed, the **lucky** gal got to marry Steve. If she failed, the wedding was off. (Happily, she passed.) We certainly hope that kind of thing doesn't happen in **real** life. But say it did. Suppose some *Simpsons* fan decided to quiz his/her betrothed on movies, Rolling Stones albums, and **episodes** of *ALF* before making it legal. It could happen. That's why we wanted to put this **warning** up front: Pop-culture-crazy people, please don't make your potential lifemates pass the quizzes in this book. You might end up **alone** forever. We're not fooling around here. We've included a few beginner's-level questions just to keep your **spirits** up, but a lot of these queries are truly tough. We're talking Lee Marvin **tough**, not Orlando Bloom tough. As Jack Nicholson said—in what movie?—"Are we clear?" That's right: *A Few Good Men*. See? This is **fun**. Good luck!

# The 1960s

The Beatles *Ed Sullivan* *2001: A Space Odyssey* Andy Griffith The Supremes
*Psycho* **Get Smart** *Bye Bye Birdie* *Dr. Strangelove* *Bonnie and Clyde*
Paul Revere and the Raiders *Fantastic Voyage* Young Rascals Dick Van Dyke
*Valley of the Dolls* *The Beverly Hillbillies* **The Monkees** *A Charlie
Brown Christmas* *Gilligan's Island* *The Absent-Minded Professor* *West Side
Story* *Gomer Pyle* *My Fair Lady* Velvet Underground *Sesame Street* *Family
Affair* **Alfred Hitchcock** *Mary Poppins* *It's a Mad, Mad, Mad,
Mad World* James Bond *Cleopatra* *The Jungle Book* *Laugh In* *The Flying Nun*
*Mission: Impossible* Woodstock *The Jetsons* *Batman* *Bewitched* *To Kill a
Mockingbird* *Raindrops Keep Fallin' on My Head* *I Dream of Jeannie* *The Pink
Panther* Carole King *Beach Blanket Bingo* **The Graduate** The Who
*The Addams Family* *Jonny Quest* *Lawrence of Arabia* Three Dog Night

**1** On The Andy Griffith Show, Barney Fife (Don Knotts) was Sheriff Taylor's deputy and also his ___.

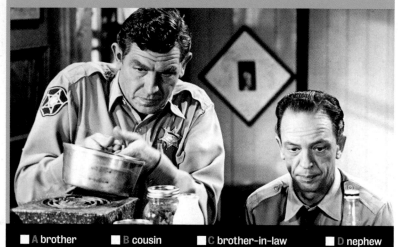

☐ A brother ☐ B cousin ☐ C brother-in-law ☐ D nephew

**2** In 1968's *2001: A Space Odyssey*, what song could the HAL 9000 computer sing?

**3** In the 1963 film musical *Bye Bye Birdie*, what's the name of the song Conrad Birdie (Jesse Pearson) is supposed to sing to Sweet Apple, Ohio, teen Kim McAfee (Ann-Margret) on *The Ed Sullivan Show*?

**4** Who was the original Supreme, heard on such hits as "Baby Love" and "Come See About Me," who was replaced in the trio by Cindy Birdsong in 1967?

A. Florence Ballard
B. Kaye Ballard
C. Caroll Ballard
D. Mary Wilson

**5** On *Get Smart*, Maxwell Smart (Don Adams) worked for CONTROL, but what was the name of the evil agency he was out to defeat?

**6** A further challenge of your knowledge of *Get Smart*: Complete this Maxwell Smart signature expression: "Would you ___?"

**7** The legendary Spencer Tracy died in 1967, just weeks after completing work on this, his last film.

**8** The assassination of what political leader prompted the Academy of Motion Picture Arts and Sciences to postpone the Academy Awards ceremony for two days in 1968?

**9** In 1961's *The Absent-Minded Professor*, bumbling scientist Ned Brainard (Fred MacMurray) invents Flubber. What combination of words makes up the word "Flubber"?

# 10

**In 1960's** Psycho**, how much money does Marion Crane (**Janet Leigh**) make off with?**

Answer:

7

1. Paul Lynde

2. David White

# 11

Match these characters from TV's *Bewitched* to the actors who portrayed them:

A. Samantha    B. Endora
C. Uncle Arthur    D. Larry Tate

3. Elizabeth Montgomery

4. Agnes Moorehead

**12** While we're on the subject of *Bewitched*, name the two actors who played Darrin.

**13** How long did viewers wait for Lucille Ball to return in a half-hour TV sitcom between *I Love Lucy* and *The Lucy Show*?

A. 2 years
B. 1 year
C. 10 years
D. 5 years

**14** The Emmy-winning 1969–'70 comedy *My World and Welcome to It* was based on what writer's life?

**15** Complete this lyric to the *Gilligan's Island* theme:
*The mate was a mighty sailing man, The skipper brave and sure. Five passengers set sail that day ___.*

**16** What musical question do Simon & Garfunkel ask of Joe DiMaggio in the song "Mrs. Robinson"?

Answer:

## 17 Who did the Monkees musically ask to "cheer up" in their single "Daydream Believer"?

Answer:

**21** How much does Lucy charge Charlie Brown for counseling sessions in 1965's *A Charlie Brown Christmas*?
A. 5¢
B. 10¢
C. 25¢
D. $1

**22** In 1961's *West Side Story* and in 1964's *My Fair Lady*, whose singing voice subbed in for star Natalie Wood as Maria and Audrey Hepburn as Eliza Doolittle?

**18** Name the first number 1 hit by blue-eyed soul band the Young Rascals in 1966, which was a cover of an R&B tune by the Olympics.

A. "How Can I Be Sure"
B. "Good Lovin'"
C. "People Got to Be Free"
D. "A Beautiful Morning"

**19** Peter Sellers played three different roles in the 1964 satiric masterpiece *Dr. Strangelove or: How I Learned to Stop Worrying and Love the Bomb*. Which of these is NOT one of the characters he portrayed?
A. Group Captain Lionel Mandrake
B. Major T. J. "King" Kong
C. President Merkin Muffley
D. Dr. Strangelove

**20** *Gomer Pyle, U.S.M.C.*, starring Jim Nabors as Private Pyle, was a spin-off of what TV series?

**23** Speaking of *My Fair Lady*, what is the phrase Eliza Doolittle repeats and repeats to learn how proper English is spoken?

**24** *Cleopatra* stars Richard Burton and Elizabeth Taylor reunited on the big screen for the adaptation of which Edward Albee play?

# 25 Who was the frontman for rockers Paul Revere & the Raiders?
(Hint: It's not Paul Revere.)

Answer:

Classic TV Test Classic TV Test Classic

**60's**

**The Dick Van Dyke Show** starred Van Dyke and Mary Tyler Moore as young marrieds Rob and Laura Petrie.
Check your knowledge of the seminal sitcom >>>

**26** What were the names of Rob's cowriters on *The Alan Brady Show* (as played by Morey Amsterdam and Rose Marie)?

**27** In what town do the Petries live?
A. Scarsdale, New York
B. Nutley, New Jersey
C. New Rochelle, New York
D. New York, New York

**28** TRUE OR FALSE? Rob always tripped over the ottoman in the opening credits.

**29** Who were the Petries' neighbors and closest friends?

Answer:

## 30 What term did TV's *Beverly Hillbillies* use to describe their mansion's beautiful swimming pool?

Answer:

**35** Name the very English gentleman's gentleman who was the butler/nanny on the '60s-era TV series *Family Affair*.

### 36 BONUS
Who were his charges?

**37** What band did Graham Nash belong to before joining Crosby, Stills and Nash?

**38** Which TV western series featured a theme song that urged listeners to "Move 'em on, head 'em up, Head 'em up, move 'em out"?
A. *Bonanza*
B. *Gunsmoke*
C. *Rawhide*
D. *Chuckwagon Theater*

**39** Name the James Bond nemesis who used a bowler hat with a razor-sharp brim as a weapon.

**31** What's wrong with the title of the 1969 disaster flick *Krakatoa, East of Java*?

**32** What Andy Warhol darling sang alongside Lou Reed in the Velvet Underground? (Hint: She was also the subject of a 1995 documentary.)

**33** Which comic did NOT appear in 1963's *It's a Mad, Mad, Mad, Mad World*?
A. Milton Berle
B. Phil Silvers
C. Sid Caesar
D. Buddy Hackett
E. Desi Arnaz

**34** According to Scott McKenzie's 1967 hit song, you should wear flowers in your hair if you're going to this city.

1. Who's Afraid of Virginia Woolf?

2. Planet of the Apes

# 40

## Match the memorable dialogue to its '60s-era film:

A. "It's a madhouse, a madhouse!"   B. "Total war"

C. "I'm a bagel on a plate full of onion rolls!"

D. "Gentlemen, you can't fight in here! This is the war room"

3. Dr. Strangelove

4. Funny Girl

# 41

In The Jetsons' theme song, whom do you meet after George Jetson?

Elroy
**A.**

Jane
**B.**

Judy
**C.**

Astro
**D.**

Answer:

**42** In 1967's *The Jungle Book*, Mowgli is a
A. bear
B. snake
C. boy
D. monkey

**43** Name the quiet coastal town that Melanie Daniels (Tippi Hedren) drives to in the 1963 Alfred Hitchcock thriller *The Birds*.

**44** Faye Dunaway earned her first Oscar nomination for what 1967 shoot-'em-up?

**45** What 1960 Italian film introduced the word *paparazzi* to the language, derived from its photographer character Paparazzo?

**46** Before she was the unusually gifted Sister Bertrille on *The Flying Nun*, Sally Field was an unusually perky TV teen on this film series turned sitcom.

**47** The 1964 film Mary Poppins is based on the best-selling books of what author?

A  A. A. Milne    B  E. B. White    C  P. L. Travers    D  J. K. Rowling

**48** On The Bullwinkle Show, where did Rocky and Bullwinkle live?

Answer:
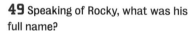

**49** Speaking of Rocky, what was his full name?

**50** What's the title of the 1961 best seller—about an infant boy born on Mars and brought back to Earth— that brought the term "grok" into everyday language?

**51** Which household did Hazel (Shirley Booth) rule with an iron fist?
A. the Johnsons
B. the Baxters
C. the Stevenses
D. the Stones

**52** Complete this well-known introduction from the '60s–'70s TV series Mission: Impossible: "...As always, should you or any member of your I.M. Force be caught or killed, the secretary will disavow all knowledge of your actions. This ___."

**53** Jackie Gleason was nominated for only one Oscar throughout his career. Name the 1961 drama for which he earned a best supporting actor nod.

**54** The four main characters in Jackie Gleason's The Honeymooners later became the prototypes for the main characters of what '60s-era animated series?

**55** In a 1967 Bobbie Gentry hit song, who jumped off the Tallahatchie Bridge?

**56** Burgess Meredith was which Batman villain on the '60s-era TV series?
A. the Riddler
B. the Joker
C. the Penguin
D. Mr. Freeze

**57** In the film title Valley of the Dolls, what are "dolls"?

1. The Chantels

2. The Ronettes

# 58 Match the pop hit to the '60s-era group that performed it:

A. "Be My Baby"  B. "He's So Fine"
C. "Maybe"  D. "Leader of the Pack"

3. The Chiffons

4. The Shangri-Las

# 59

The miniaturized crew of 1966's sci-fi classic **Fantastic Voyage** were injected into a scientist's bloodstream to do what in his brain?

- ■ A. remove a bullet
- ■ B. remove a blood clot
- ■ C. remove a tumor
- ■ D. remove a bone fragment

**60** Where did *To Kill a Mockingbird*'s Jem and Scout find odd...gifts?

**61** Name the British Invasion band that had a hit in 1965 with "Mrs. Brown You've Got a Lovely Daughter."

**62** BONUS
Name the band's frontman.

**63** What do Secret Squirrel and Bugs Bunny have in common?

**64** On I Dream of Jeannie, where did Jeannie (Barbara Eden) and Major Nelson (Larry Hagman) live?

Answer:

# Ultimate Fan Challenge:

## Hey, dude, test your knowledge of Beatles trivia.

**1.** What song did the band open with on its first *Ed Sullivan Show* appearance in 1964?
A. "I Want to Hold Your Hand"
B. "She Loves You"
C. "A Hard Day's Night"
D. "All My Loving"

**2.** He was the Beatles' original drummer, before Ringo Starr joined in 1962.

**3.** TRUE OR FALSE? Beatle Paul McCartney's real first name is James.

**4.** In what English town did the Beatles begin playing together?

**5.** Name their four feature films.

**6.** Who was the first Beatle to appear in a feature film without his bandmates?

**7.** "Yesterday" is one of the most famous songs of all time, but what did Paul McCartney originally have the lyrics say?

**8.** Whom did John Lennon once casually remark the Beatles were bigger than, which resulted in the public burning of the band's records?

**9.** Who was the original Beatles member who died in 1962, before the band became famous?
A. Stuart Sutcliffe
B. Stuart Little
C. Stuart Townsend
D. Stuart Elliott

**10.** What was the last Beatles album recorded?

# The Beatles

# 65

**In the mid-1960s, Ted Nugent started out with what band?**

- ◼ (A.) Terry Knight and the Pack
- ◼ (B.) Bob Seger and the Silver Bullet Band
- ◼ (C.) the Amboy Dukes
- ◼ (D.) MC5

**66** What was the name of the pop-rock-variety show that aired from 1965 to 1966 and featured such revolving hosts as Paul Anka and Frankie Avalon?

A. *Hullabaloo*
B. *The Bugaloos*
C. *Pop!*
D. *Music, Music, Music*

**67 NAME THAT TUNE**
This theme song, written by Harry Nilsson, accompanied what 1969 TV series?
"People let me tell you 'bout my best friend. He's a one boy cuddly toy. My up, my down, my pride and joy."

**68** What is Inspector Clouseau's first name in *The Pink Panther*?
A. Hercule
B. Gilles
C. Jean-Claude
D. Jacques

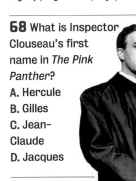

**69** Who composed the Three Dog Night top 10 hit "One"?

■ A Harry Nilsson    ■ B Laura Nyro    ■ C Fred Neil    ■ D Neil Diamond

**70** What were Bonnie and Clyde's last names?

**71** B. J. Thomas's 1969 number 1 hit "Raindrops Keep Fallin' on My Head" was the theme song to what film?

**72** Who recorded a top 5 song that was written or cowritten by Carole King?
A. the Shirelles
B. the Monkees
C. the Drifters
D. Little Eva
E. all of the above

**73** Name the 1969 Foundations hit that featured this lyric:
"You were my toy but I could be the boy you adore. If you'd just let me know (bah-dah-dah). Although you're untrue, I'm attracted to you all the more. Why do I need you so?"

**74** What are the two words most often uttered by towering butler Lurch (Ted Cassidy) on TV's The Addams Family?

Answer:

**75** What early-'60s sitcom featured *The Munsters'* Al Lewis and *The Facts of Life*'s Charlotte Rae as husband and wife?

**76** Put these famous '60s-era "beach" movies in order of release.
A. *Beach Party*
B. *Beach Blanket Bingo*
C. *Bikini Beach*

**77 BONUS**
Name these films' two beach-lovin' costars.

**78 TRUE OR FALSE?** Jonny Quest's dog was named Hadji.

**79** When Benjamin (Dustin Hoffman) checks into the hotel for his first tryst with Mrs. Robinson (Anne Bancroft) in 1967's *The Graduate*, what does he say his name is?

# 80

## Who was Big Bird's best friend—who no one believed existed—in the early days of *Sesame Street*?

■ A. Oscar the Grouch

■ B. Roosevelt Franklin

■ C. Snuffleupagus

■ D. Cookie Monster

1. DeForest Kelley

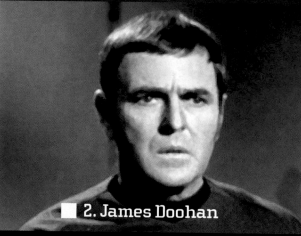

2. James Doohan

# 81

Match the actor to the officer of the USS Enterprise he or she portrayed on the original Star Trek TV series:

A. Lt. Commander Scott  B. Lt. Sulu
C. Lt. Uhura  D. Lt. Commander McCoy

3. George Takei

4. Nichelle Nichols

**82** More names to know from *The Graduate*: Who is the man Elaine (Katharine Ross) intends to marry before Benjamin rescues her? (Hint: Benjamin meets him at the zoo.)

A. Carl Sanders
B. Carl Smith
C. Carl Sinclair
D. Carl Spier

**83** *Lawrence of Arabia* took home seven Oscars at the 1963 Academy Award ceremonies, but star Peter O'Toole did not win best actor. Who did?

A. Burt Lancaster
B. Jack Lemmon
C. Marcello Mastroianni
D. Gregory Peck

**84** The 1965 William Shatner film *Incubus*, about a strange island inhabited by demons, was filmed in what language?

A. Latin
B. Esperanto
C. Spanish
D. Etruscan

**85** In 1961's Breakfast at Tiffany's, what is Holly Golightly's (Audrey Hepburn) pet cat's name?

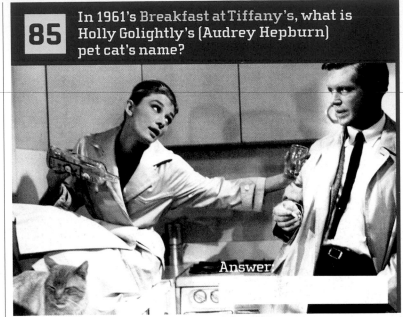

Answer

**86** What classical work was comedian Allan Sherman's parody tune "Hello Muddah, Hello Fadduh!" based on?
A. Strauss's *The Blue Danube*
B. Ponchielli's *Dance of the Hours*
C. Rossini's *William Tell Overture*
D. Debussy's *La Mer*

**87** What future rock star was turned down to join the Monkees?
A. Jim Morrison
B. Stephen Stills
C. Neil Diamond
D. Paul Simon

**88** In 1967's *Barefoot in the Park*, where did newlyweds Paul and Corie Bratter (Robert Redford and Jane Fonda) spend their honeymoon?

**89** Name the actor who succeeded Andy Griffith in 1968, when his *Andy Griffith Show* became *Mayberry R.F.D.*

1960 1970 1980 1990 2000

## 90 In what New York State town did the 1969 Woodstock festival take place?

■ A Woodstock    ■ B New Paltz    ■ C Saugerties    ■ D Bethel

**91** What was the name of the French poodle that accompanied novelist John Steinbeck on his trip across America?
A. Millie
B. Buddy
C. Ernest
D. Charley

**92** Where did Ernest Hemmingway die?
A. Idaho
B. Cuba
C. Key West
D. Spain

**93** Which Paul Newman movie contains the famous line, "What we've got here is failure to communicate"?
A. *Hud*
B. *The Hustler*
C. *Cool Hand Luke*
D. *Butch Cassidy and the Sundance Kid*

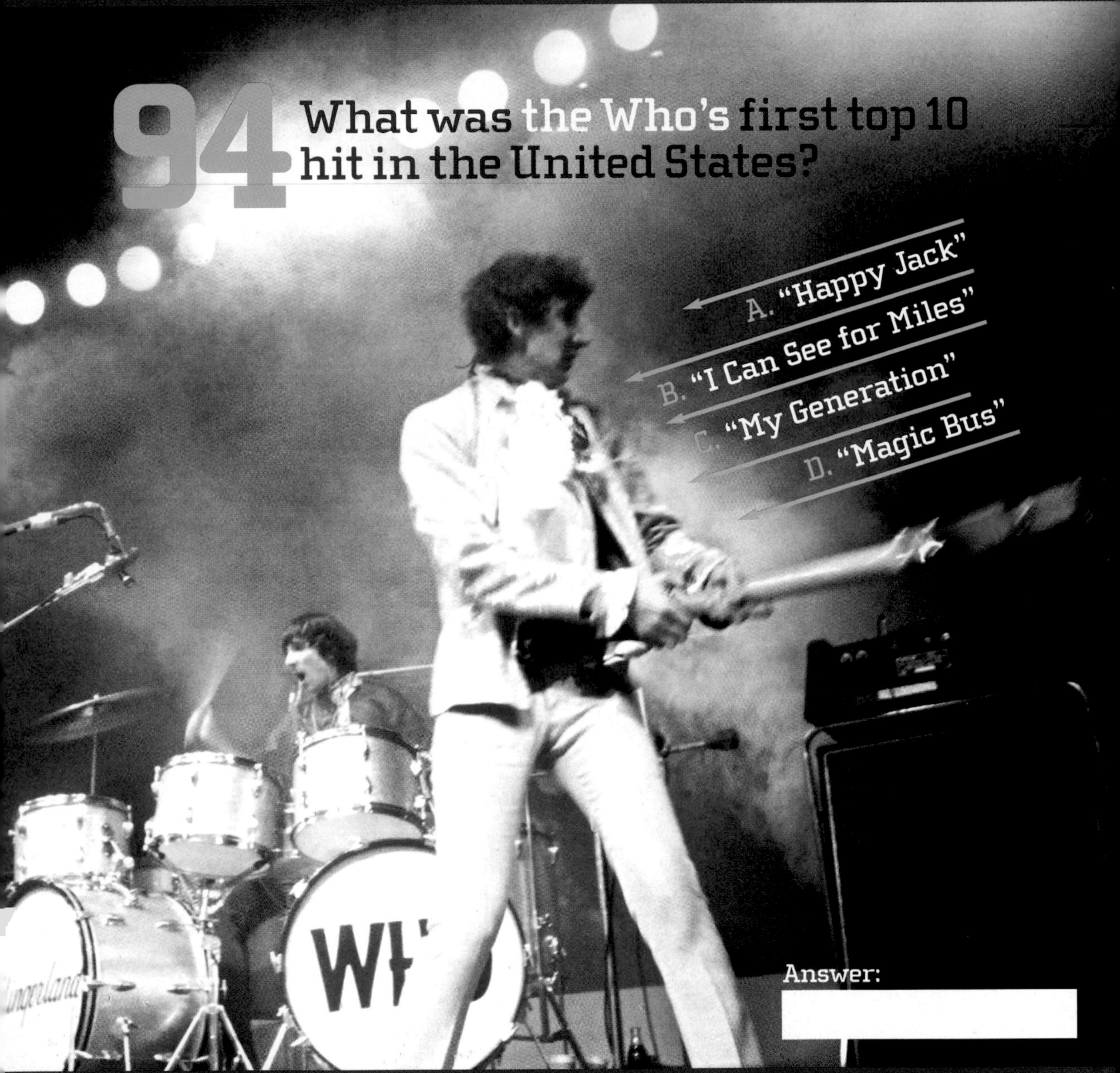

# 94

## What was the Who's first top 10 hit in the United States?

A. "Happy Jack"

B. "I Can See for Miles"

C. "My Generation"

D. "Magic Bus"

Answer:

60's Test Classic TV Test Classic TV Test Classic TV

# Five trivia challenges about the comedy-variety series Rowan & Martin's Laugh-In

**95** What was the name of Lily Tomlin's telephone-operator character?

**96** Whom did she call?

**97** What was her catchphrase?

**98** What presidential candidate appeared on the show to say, "Sock it to me"?

**99** What was the name of Tomlin's young-girl-in-a-big-rocker character?

Answer:

## 100 Did Dr. Richard Kimble (David Janssen) ever catch the one-armed man on the TV series The Fugitive?

Answer:

**104** Ann-Margret costarred with Elvis Presley in which 1964 race-car romance?

**105** Which actress NEVER played Catwoman on the *Batman* TV series?
A. Lee Meriwether
B. Eartha Kitt
C. Mitzi Gaynor
D. Julie Newmar

**106** Who was Talky Tina?

**107** Before they were famous, under what name did the future Simon & Garfunkel release their records?

**108** I played James Bond in 1969's *On Her Majesty's Secret Service*. Who am I?

**109** Which band censored its lyrics when appearing on *The Ed Sullivan Show*?
A. the Doors
B. the Rolling Stones
C. the Yardbirds
D. the Beatles

**101** In the 1968 film *Yours, Mine and Ours*, starring Lucille Ball and Henry Fonda, what future *Animal House* frat boy played the oldest son?
A. Peter Riegert
B. Tim Matheson
C. Tom Hulce
D. Stephen Furst

**102** In what town did both the sitcoms *Green Acres* and *Petticoat Junction* take place?

**103** Name the 1963 Elizabeth Taylor epic that's notable for being one of the most expensive films of all time.

■ A. The Beatles

■ B. The Rolling Stones

# 110

While we're on the subject of pop stars on The Ed Sullivan Show, which of these bands appeared most frequently?

■ C. Herman's Hermits

■ D. The Dave Clark Five

■ 1. Father Knows Best

■ 2. Leave It to Beaver

# 111

## Match the sitcom with its fictional city: A. Hilldale  B. Central City  C. Mayfield D. Springfield

■ 3. The Donna Reed Show

■ 4. The Many Loves of Dobie Gillis

# 112 What are the secret identities of Batman and Robin?

Answer:

## 113 What color set Tippi Hedren off in the 1964 Alfred Hitchcock thriller *Marnie*?

☐ A Red ☐ B Green ☐ C Purple ☐ D Black

**117** What put TV's hard-nosed Detective *Ironside* (Raymond Burr) in a wheelchair?
A. polio
B. car accident
C. amputation
D. a would-be assassin's bullet

**118** Robert Preston won a Tony playing con man Harold Hill in Broadway's *The Music Man*. But who did the studio originally want for the role when it went to the big screen in 1962?
A. Elvis Presley
B. Cary Grant
C. Frank Sinatra
D. Peter O'Toole

**115** In 1968, NBC cut away from a football game (New York Jets vs. Oakland Raiders) with sixty-five seconds to go and missed its upset ending to show this movie.

**116** Where are Joe Buck (Jon Voight) and Ratso Rizzo (Dustin Hoffman) located in the last scene of 1969's *Midnight Cowboy*?
A. New York
B. Texas
C. Georgia
D. Florida

**114** Before he captained *The Love Boat* and before he was a news writer in *The Mary Tyler Moore Show*, Gavin MacLeod was a cast member of what seafaring '60s sitcom?

**119** What real-life bluegrass band portrayed the Darling family on *The Andy Griffith Show*?
A. the Carter Family
B. the Country Gentlemen
C. the Dillards
D. the Osborne Brothers

# 120

In 1965's
The
Sound of
Music,
just how
many Von
Trapp
children
are there?

A. Five
B. Six
C. Seven
D. Ten

Answer:

# The 1970s

Woody Allen *One Flew Over the Cuckoo's Nest*  *Short People*  *Love Story*

*Three's Company*  **Blazing Saddles**  *Superman: The Movie*

*Little House on the Prairie*  Bruce Springsteen  *The Poseidon Adventure*

*Nashville*  *Close Encounters of the Third Kind*  Gladys Knight and the Pips

*The Brady Bunch*  *Mary Tyler Moore*  **The Odd Couple**  *Kojak*

*Love Story*  *Good Times*  *Young Frankenstein*  *The Partridge Family*  *M*A*S*H*

*Monday Night Football*  Flip Wilson  *One Day at a Time*  *The Bionic Woman*

*Monty Python*  **Charlie's Angels**  *All in the Family*  *Animal House*

*The Godfather*  *Taxi*  *Chico and the Man*  *Five Easy Pieces*  *Happy Days*

*The Stepford Wives*  *Baretta*  Joni Mitchell  *Mork & Mindy*  Patti Smith  *Alien*

*Heaven Can Wait*  *Willy Wonka & the Chocolate Factory*  Eagles  *Star Wars*

*The Towering Inferno*  *Earthquake*  **The Exorcist**  *Barney Miller*

## 1

**Who sang 1972's** The Poseidon Adventure's **Academy Award-winning song "The Morning After"?**

**Answer:**

**2** In 1975's *One Flew Over the Cuckoo's Nest*, what does McMurphy (Jack Nicholson) want to watch on television in the asylum?

**3** Who played the original landlord, Mr. Roper, on *Three's Company*?
A. Don Knotts
B. Norman Fell
C. Pat Harrington
D. Richard Masur

**4** While we're on the subject of *Three's Company*, which replacement roommate "came and knocked" on their door last: Suzanne Somers, Jenilee Harrison, or Priscilla Barnes?

**5** Members of which band sang on Randy Newman's hit 1977 single "Short People"?
A. Fleetwood Mac
B. Eagles
C. The Bee Gees
D. The Beach Boys

**6** Which actor gives a wordless performance as a tricycle-riding magician in Robert Altman's 1975 film, *Nashville*?

A. Jeff Goldblum
B. Chevy Chase
C. William Shatner
D. Richard Dreyfuss

**7** TRUE OR FALSE? Gig Young was originally cast to play the Waco Kid in Mel Brooks's 1974 hit *Blazing Saddles* before Gene Wilder took the role.

**8** Which one of the Ingalls girls went blind on *Little House on the Prairie*?

**9** Which was NOT the name of one of Bruce Springsteen's bands?
A. Dr. Zoom and the Sonic Boom
B. Child
C. Steel Mill
D. The Question

■ 1. Eric Idle

■ 2. John Cleese

# 10

**Match the Monty Python troupe member with the character he was best known for:** A. Dennis Moore   B. Mr. Pithers
C. Mr. Smoke-Too-Much   D. SPAM Waitress

■ 3. Michael Palin

■ 4. Terry Jones

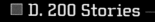

D. 200 Stories

# 11
## How tall is The Towering Inferno?

C. 138 stories
B. 135 stories

A. 100 stories

**12** Gladys Knight & the Pips charted smash hit after smash hit, but only this 1973 single actually reached number 1 on the *Billboard* pop chart.

**13** Name the character played by a young James Brolin in the '70s series *Marcus Welby, M.D.*

**14** I accompanied rising star Bette Midler as a pianist and arranger in the early '70s before becoming a singer-songwriter in my own right with a string of 25 Top 40 hits. Who am I?

**15** John Cazale played Al Pacino's brother Fredo in the *Godfather* movies. Name the other '70s drama that featured the two actors holding the police at bay.

**16** **TRUE OR FALSE?** Steve Martin was one of the original Not Ready for Prime Time Players on Saturday Night Live.

Answer:

**17** On an episode of *The Mary Tyler Moore Show*, what somber event made Mary laugh?

Answer:

**22** Name the Inez and Charlie Foxx tune that James Taylor and Carly Simon made into a new top 10 duet hit in 1974.

**23** Who was worried about her "taffeta, darling" in the 1974 Mel Brooks spoof *Young Frankenstein*?

**24** Wait, more on *Young Frankenstein*: Who played the blind hermit who was going to "make espresso"?

**18** Name the 1978 ballad cowritten by punker Patti Smith and rocker Bruce Springsteen. (Hint: It was also a hit for 10,000 Maniacs in the '90s.)

**19** Oscar Madison (Jack Klugman) was a sportswriter. But what did Felix Unger (Tony Randall) do for a living on TV's *The Odd Couple*?

**20** What real-life musical family was the basis for TV's *The Partridge Family*?

**21** What Ivy League universities did the lovers of 1970's *Love Story* (Ryan O'Neal and Ali MacGraw) attend?
A. Harvard and Radcliffe
B. Yale and Princeton
C. Harvard and Cornell
D. Harvard and Yale

**25** What did John Belushi's Bluto from 1978's *Animal House* become, according to the closing credits?
A. congressman
B. senator
C. president of a large corporation
D. dean of a university

A. Elton John

B. Tiny Tim

# 26 Which singer's real name was Herbert Khaury?

C. Freddie Mercury

D. Kinky Friedman

Classic TV Test Classic TV Test
70's

How much do you know about
The Brady Bunch?

Take this BB challenge>>>

**27** How did the Brady kids' house of cards finally fall?

A. Marcia flipped her hair on it.

B. Tiger crashed through it.

C. Bobby threw a ball at it.

D. Alice spilled gravy on it.

**28** Who were the Brady's rarely seen neighbors?

**29** What was the name of Cindy's favorite doll?

A. Kitty KarryAll

B. Miss Kitty

C. Chatty Kathy

D. Mrs. Beasly

**30** What was the name of Carol's cute nephew who joined the show in later seasons?

A. Dill

B. Ernie

C. Oliver

D. Chip

**31** On the opening credits, who was the center square?

**32** Who was Alice's steady beau? (Hint: He was the Bradys' butcher.)

Answer:

## 33 Who was the first cast member of *All in the Family* to win an Emmy?

Answer:

**39** In the original *King Kong*, the big ape perishes by falling from New York's Empire State Building. Where does he fall from in the 1976 remake, starring Jessica Lange?

**40** What was Joe Pendleton's (Warren Beatty) occupation—before he died and came back in the body of a millionaire—in 1978's *Heaven Can Wait*?
A. NBA star
B. pro football quarterback
C. golf pro
D. hockey goalie

**34** Also on *All in the Family*, what was Meathead's relationship to Archie Bunker?

**35** A further test of your *Animal House* knowledge: What were the names of the rival fraternities?

**36** What was the name of Tony Baretta's (Robert Blake) pet cockatoo?
A. Albert
B. Amadeus
C. Fred
D. Elvis

**37** Howard Cosell appeared as himself in which two Woody Allen movies?

**38** Who was nicknamed "the Master of Disaster" in the 1970s?

**41** Name the meddlesome, tool-belt-toting superintendent who kept a watchful eye on the women of TV's *One Day at a Time*.

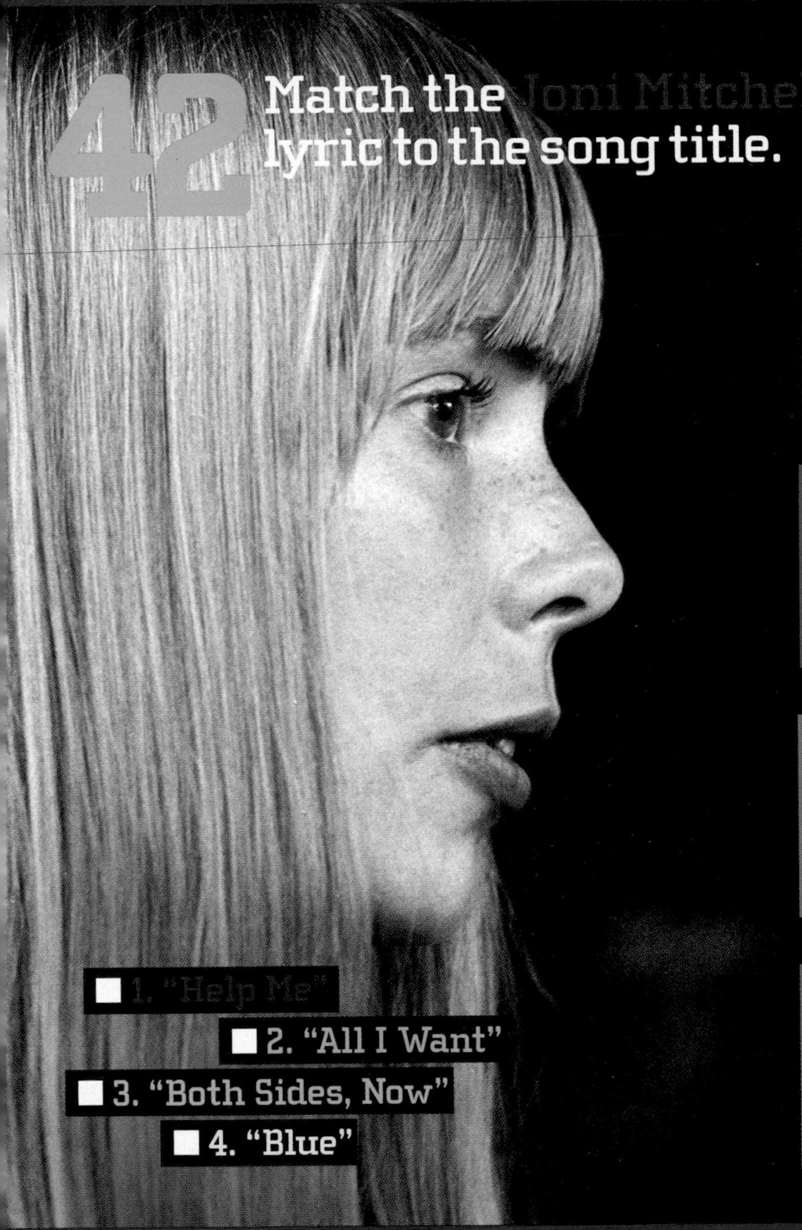

# 42

## Match the Joni Mitchell lyric to the song title.

A. "Everybody's saying that hell's the hippest way to go/Well, I don't think so..."

B. "Moons and Junes and Ferris wheels/The dizzy dancing way that you feel"

C. "You dance with the lady/With the hole in her stocking/Didn't it feel good"

D. "Alive, alive, I want to get up and jive/I want to wreck my stockings in some juke box dive"

☐ 1. "Help Me"

☐ 2. "All I Want"

☐ 3. "Both Sides, Now"

☐ 4. "Blue"

1. Hawkeye Pierce

2. Sherman Potter

# 43 Match the M*A*S*H character with his home state:

A. Missouri    B. Indiana

C. Maine     D. California

3. B. J. Hunnicut

4. Frank Burns

**44** Also on TV's *M*A*S*H*, what were the nasty nicknames for Major Houlihan (Loretta Swit) and Major Burns (Larry Linville)?

**45** What *M*A*S*H* character was played by Gary Burghoff in both the 1970 film and the subsequent TV series?

**46** What movie do Al Pacino and Diane Keaton go to see at Radio City Music Hall (the night Don Corleone is shot) in 1972's *The Godfather*? (Hint: They have a conversation about the film as they are leaving the theater.)
A. *The Bells of St. Mary's*
B. *Blithe Spirit*
C. *Brief Encounter*
D. *The Clock*

**47** Most of the time, he was just "the Fonz," but what was the *Happy Days* regular's real first name?

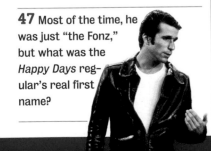

**48** On The Flip Wilson Show, who was sassy Geraldine Jones's jealous boyfriend?

■ A Leroy    ■ B Crazy Eyes    ■ C Killer    ■ D Melvin

**49** What fictional resort island was the setting for the Steven Spielberg thriller Jaws?

Answer:

**50** More on *Happy Days*: Who played Arnold?

**51** Which of these TV shows was NOT a '70s-era hit for *All in the Family* producer Norman Lear?
A. *Sanford and Son*
B. *Maude*
C. *Rhoda*
D. *One Day at a Time*

**52** How many seasons did Farrah Fawcett spend on *Charlie's Angels?*

**53** Nick Nolte and Peter Strauss played brothers at odds in what 1976 soap opera miniseries?

**54** The man now known as Yusuf Islam was this '70s-era singer-songwriter.

**55** Freddie Prinze was Chico, but who was Ed Brown, aka "the man," in *Chico and the Man*?

A. Ed Asner
B. Jack Albertson
C. Redd Foxx
D. Mickey Rooney

**56** Nicole Kidman starred as the unsuspecting new suburbanite Joanna Eberhart in the recent remake of *The Stepford Wives*. Who originated the role in 1975?

**57** Which U.S. president played at Nashville's Grand Ole Opry?
A. Ronald Reagan
B. Richard Nixon
C. Bill Clinton
D. Jimmy Carter

**58** Who appeared on the inaugural cover of *People* magazine in 1974?
A. Faye Dunaway
B. Goldie Hawn
C. Jacqueline Onassis
D. Mia Farrow

A. A Clockwork Orange

B. Cabaret

# 59 Which 1970 movie ends with the line, "I was cured, all right"?

C. One Flew Over the Cuckoo's Nest

D. Marathon Man

# 60

## On TV's Taxi, what was the secret ingredient to Latka's (Andy Kaufman) irresistible cookies?

Answer:

**61** Speaking of *Taxi*, where did all the cabbies work?

**62** This album earned a famed songwriter superstar status and stayed on the charts for almost six years.

**63** Fill in the lyric to this Neil Young tune: "Tin soldiers and __ 's coming."

**64** What '70s mock talk show starred Martin Mull and Fred Willard?

**65** What singer was Bette Midler's 1979 film *The Rose* based on?

**66** Who was The Bionic Woman's (Lindsay Wagner) bionic pooch?

| ■ A Minnie | ■ B Max | ■ C Monkey | ■ D Mickey |

# Ultimate Fan Challenge:

You liked his movies—especially the early, funny ones. Here are ten tests of trivia about Woody Allen's '70s classics.

**1.** In 1973's *Sleeper*, Allen is Miles Monroe, a health-food store owner who's cryogenically frozen and defrosted 200 years later. Among the gizmos of Miles's futuristic new world is a mechanical dog. What's his name?
A. Fido
B. Rex
C. Rags
D. Buddy

**2.** This quote is from the opening speech for which Allen film? "Chapter One. He was as tough and romantic as the city he loved. Behind his black-rimmed glasses was the coiled sexual power of a jungle cat. I love this."

**3.** What real-life media theorist was pulled into the frame to help Alvy Singer (Allen again) prove his point to a boorish professor in 1977's *Annie Hall*?

**4.** In 1971's *Bananas*, Woody Allen is Fielding Mellish, a nebbish who falls in love with a political activist. What country does Fielding run off to and become president of?
A. San Tropez
B. San Marcos
C. San Salvador
D. San José

**5.** In 1975's *Love and Death*, Allen's parody of Russian literature and Ingmar Bergman films, what does Sonja (Diane Keaton) make a meatloaf out of?

**6.** Which Woody Allen film first paired Allen and Diane Keaton?

**7.** In 1979's *Manhattan*, for whom did Isaac Davis's wife leave him?

**8. BONUS**
What actress played the ex-wife?

**9.** Name the only '70s-era film that Allen wrote and directed but did not act in.

**10.** What is the last line in *Annie Hall*?
A. "I'm into leather."
B. "Whaddya want, it was my first play."
C. "Yeah, and such small portions."
D. "Most of us need the eggs."

**11.** In 1978 and 1979, Allen was nominated for five Academy Awards, but how many Oscars did he actually win?
A. five
B. four
C. three
D. two

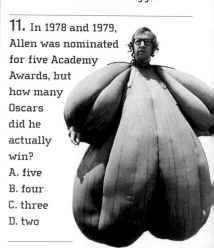

# Woody Allen

# 67

In 1971's Willy Wonka & the Chocolate Factory, how many golden tickets were there, and who found them?

Answer:

**68** What was the British title of Nick Lowe's *Pure Pop for Now People* album?
A. *I Love Everyone*
B. *The Rose of England*
C. *Jesus of Cool*
D. *Cruel to Be Kind*

**69** The phrase "jump the shark" refers to a defining moment in a TV series's life—when the show has reached its peak and is now sliding downhill. Name the '70s sitcom that inspired the phrase.

**70** Emmylou Harris got her big break in the early '70s backing which country-rock singer?
A. Gary Stewart
B. Gene Clark
C. Gram Parsons
D. David Allan Coe

**71** What was Neil Young's filmmaking alias?

A Bernard Fripp
B Bernard Shakey
C Bernard Charles
D Alan Smithee

**72** Name the Good Times character who made "Dy-no-mite!" a catchphrase.

Answer:

**73** What silent film star accepted an honorary Oscar in 1972 by quietly saying, "Words are so futile, so feeble"? Was it Charlie Chaplin, Harold Lloyd, or Buster Keaton?

**74** Which did Dustin Hoffman thank in his acceptance speech after he won a best actor Golden Globe for 1979's *Kramer vs. Kramer*?
A. Meryl Streep
B. his mom
C. his agent
D. divorce

**75** In 1977's *Star Wars*, what were the names of Luke Skywalker's (Mark Hamill) aunt and uncle?

**76** In the 1974 made-for-TV cheese movie *Bad Ronald*, why is Ronald (Scott Jacoby) holed up in a secret room?

**77** What sporting event was the focus of the con in 1973's *The Sting*?

A. football
B. horse racing
C. dog racing
D. the Olympics

**78** Both the Eagles and the Emotions had hits with songs called "Best of My Love." Which came first?

**79** The 1979 chiller *Alien* stranded a crew of astronauts in outer space with a deadly entity aboard ship. What is the name of the computer that controls that ship?

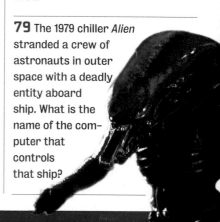

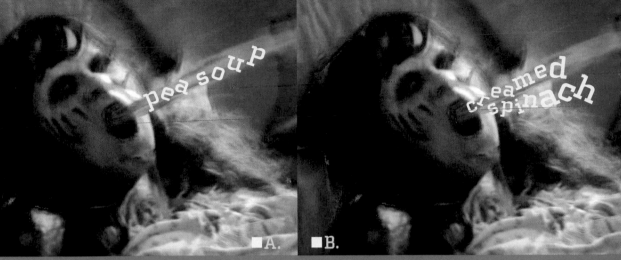

pea soup

creamed spinach

■A. ■B.

# 80 What verdant edible spewed forth during Regan's (Linda Blair) famous vomiting scene in 1973's The Exorcist?

green Jell-O

mashed peas

■C. ■D.

# 81

**In 1978's Superman: The Movie, what newspaper does Clark Kent work for?**

Answer:

**82 BONUS**
What was Superman's Krypton name?

**83** Who was Fish's (Abe Vigoda) rarely seen wife on TV's *Barney Miller*?

A. Barbara
B. Bernice
C. Denise
D. Vera

**84** What band recorded the 1978 album *More Songs About Buildings and Food*?
A. Talking Heads
B. the B-52s
C. the Ramones
D. Devo

**85** After Vanessa Redgrave's controversial acceptance speech at the 1978 Academy Awards, who later came on stage to say, "I would like to suggest to Miss Redgrave that her winning an Academy Award is not a pivotal moment in history, does not require a proclamation, and a simple 'thank you' would have sufficed"?
A. Charlton Heston
B. Paddy Chayefsky
C. Gregory Peck
D. Jack Valenti

**86** How did Mork say good-bye at the end of every episode of *Mork & Mindy*?

Answer:

**87** On the TV cop show *Hawaii Five-O*, which aired during the '70s, who told Dano to "Book 'em!"?

Answer:

**88** A precursor to *American Idol*, this 1979–85 musical variety series hosted by Deney Terrio had celebrities judging amateurs dancing to top disco tunes.

**89** What 1974 disaster movie was nominated for a best picture Oscar?

**90** While we're on the subject of disaster movies, 1974's *Earthquake* was famous for featuring what in-theater gimmick?

**91** In what year was Jackson Browne's "Doctor My Eyes" a top 10 single?

A. 1971
B. 1972
C. 1974
D. 1976

**92** Who did NOT appear in 1973's teen-cruising classic *American Graffiti*?

A. Ron Howard
B. Wolfman Jack
C. Harrison Ford
D. Penny Marshall

**93** Who hosted the first episode of *Saturday Night Live* in 1975?
A. Steve Martin
B. Tom Hanks
C. Paul Simon
D. George Carlin

**94** In what city did Martin Scorsese's 1978 concert film *The Last Waltz* take place?

**95** What famous TV film critic bought, at auction, the white disco suit worn by John Travolta in 1977's *Saturday Night Fever*?

# 96

## More on

## *Star Wars:*

## *How does the*

## *opening crawl begin?*

Answer:

# 97

In Steven Spielberg's 1977 film, what do we learn is a Close Encounter of the Third Kind?

Answer:

Answer:
1.

Answer:
2.

# 98 Name all four of the Rolling Stones' guitarists.

Answer:
3.

Answer:
4.

# 99 What year did NFL Monday Night Football begin?

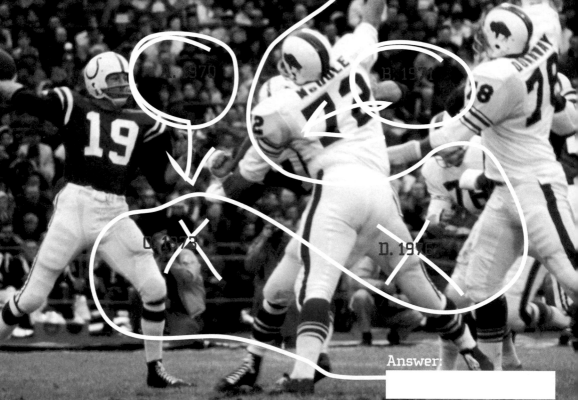

A. 1970

B. 1971

C. 1973

D. 1976

Answer:

**100 BONUS**
Who made up its first team of hosts?

**101** What 1973 rock album is purportedly synchronized with the 1939 film *The Wizard of Oz*?

**102** Who was the only employee at WJM NOT fired at the end of *The Mary Tyler Moore Show*?
A. Murray
B. Lou
C. Ted
D. Mary

**103** In 1976, I became the first female to anchor a news broadcast on a major network when I coan-chored *The ABC Evening News*. Who am I?

**104** What is the title of Patti Smith's book of poetry, published in 1978?
A. *Gloria*
B. *Sodom and Gomorrah*
C. *Babel*
D. *Easter*

**105** *Sanford and Son* ran what kind of business?
A. barber shop
B. deli
C. junkyard
D. auto repair

**106** In 1970's *Five Easy Pieces*, how does Bobby (Jack Nicholson) order his eggs?

Answer:

**107** What '70s-era TV sitcom drew criticism when its brassy leading character had an abortion?

**108** Who created TV's *The Dating Game* and *The Gong Show*?

**109** *Gunsmoke*'s Dennis Weaver returned in the '70s with this hit TV series about a rural sheriff who joins a big-city police force.

**110** After playing *The Jeffersons*' sharp-tongued maid Florence Johnston, actress Marla Gibbs got her own spin-off series. What was it called?
A. *Checking In*
B. *Check Me Out*
C. *Just Checking*
D. *Flo Jo's*

**111** What TV police detective could have been called the lolly cop?

# The 1980s

Cheers Hoosiers  The Dukes of Hazzard  Stephen King  Big  Dead Poets Society  A Different World  **Miami Vice**  Die Hard  Perfect Strangers  Tootsie  Magnum, P.I.  "Red Red Wine"  E.T.  Simon & Simon  Heathers  Airplane!  Family Ties  Michael Jackson  Some Kind of Wonderful  When Harry Met Sally  Desperately Seeking Susan  Madonna  This Is Spiñal Tap  Back to the Future  **The Brat Pack**  Blondie  Hill Street Blues  The Terminator  Live Aid  Caddyshack  The Breakfast Club  The Right Stuff  Growing Pains  Remington Steele  The Traveling Wilburys  Night Court  David Letterman  Bill & Ted's Excellent Adventure  A Flock of Seagulls  **Oprah Winfrey**  Raiders of the Lost Ark  Ghostbusters  Bull Durham  Stand by Me  The Princess Bride  Ferris Bueller's Day Off  The Cosby Show  The Color Purple  Beverly Hills Cop  The Golden Girls  Porky's  **Top Gun**  Gremlins  The A-Team  Trading Places

## 1 What school does Hickory High defeat in the Indiana state finals in 1986's *Hoosiers*?

Answer:

**2** Of the four stories collected in Stephen King's 1982 anthology *Different Seasons*, which has NOT yet been made into a feature film?
A. "Rita Hayworth and Shawshank Redemption"
B. "Apt Pupil"
C. "The Body"
D. "The Breathing Method"

**3** What real-life lawman did Kevin Costner play in 1987's *The Untouchables*?

**4** On *The Dukes of Hazzard*, what were the names of Bo and Luke's cousins—the characters who took the place of stars Tom Wopat and John Schneider for one season?

**5** Who was *Magnum, P.I.*'s (Tom Selleck) never-seen boss?

**6** BONUS
And who voiced the character?

**7** What was the Latin maxim that teacher John Keating (Robin Williams) encouraged his students to follow in 1989's *Dead Poets Society*?

**8** The *Dead Poets Society* students—including Robert Sean Leonard and Ethan Hawke—attended what fictional boarding school?
A. Wheaton Academy
B. Welton Academy
C. Wilford Academy
D. Philips Academy

**9** While we're on the subject of fictional schools, what was the name of the faux university depicted on TV's *A Different World*?

**10** BONUS
*A Different World* was a spin-off of what popular TV series?

# 11

In 1986's Ferris Bueller's Day Off, what two songs does Matthew Broderick lip-sync in the Chicago parade?

Answer:

# 12

What baseball stadium does Kevin Costner take James Earl Jones to in 1989's **Field of Dreams**?

**A** Candlestick Park

**B.** Shea Stadium

**C.** Fenway Park

**D.** Astrodome

**13** Complete this sentence, as uttered by Christian Slater in 1989's *Heathers*: "Our love is God, let's go..."
A. get a Slushie
B. get drunk
C. get a burrito
D. to church

**14** Which '80s female pop singer starred in *The Allnighter*, a film directed by her mom?
A. Susanna Hoffs of the Bangles
B. Katrina Leskanich of Katrina and the Waves
C. Belinda Carlisle of the Go-Go's
D. Chrissie Hynde of the Pretenders

**15** Philip Michael Thomas was Ricardo Tubbs, but who played Sonny Crockett's (Don Johnson) original partner on the crime series *Miami Vice*?

**16** Mork was from Ork, but where was Balki from on the '80s-era sitcom *Perfect Strangers*?

A Malki    B Maypo    C Mypos    D Pluto

## 17 On the '80s-era detective show *Simon & Simon*, the detectives were...

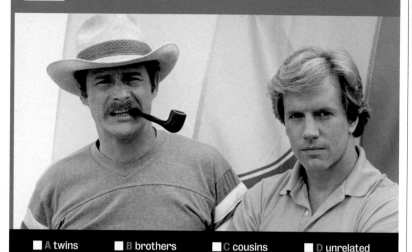

☐ **A** twins    ☐ **B** brothers    ☐ **C** cousins    ☐ **D** unrelated

**18** In the 1980s, this writer won a Pulitzer Prize *and* a best adapted screenplay Academy Award for the same work, the only time a person has ever done so.
A. Charles Fuller (for *A Soldier's Story*)
B. Beth Henley (for *Crimes of the Heart*)
C. Peter Shaffer (for *Amadeus*)
D. Alfred Uhry (for *Driving Miss Daisy*)

**19** David Leisure parlayed his gimmicky role as the lying Joe Isuzu into a full-time role on what '80s-era sitcom?

**20** Keith (Eric Stoltz) blows his college money on what in 1987's *Some Kind of Wonderful*?
A. diamond earrings
B. a Porsche
C. a trip to Vegas
D. a diamond bracelet

**21** In 1987's *Innerspace*, miniaturized Lieutenant Tuck Pendelton (Dennis Quaid) was supposed to be injected into this—but instead he ended up floating around in Jack Putter (Martin Short).
A. a bunny
B. a Chihuahua
C. a sheep
D. a chimpanzee

**22** Who was the first woman to direct a film that grossed more than $100 million?

**23** This singer-songwriter performed the Academy Award–nominated best song "It Might Be You," from 1982's *Tootsie*.

**24** In *E.T. the Extra-Terrestrial*, what future *Baywatch* babe does Elliott kiss after freeing the classroom frogs?

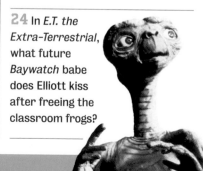

# 25

What was the name of the carnival machine that granted twelve-year-old Josh Baskin's wish in 1988's Big?

A. Zoltron

B. Zoltar

C. Zoltan

D. Zamboni

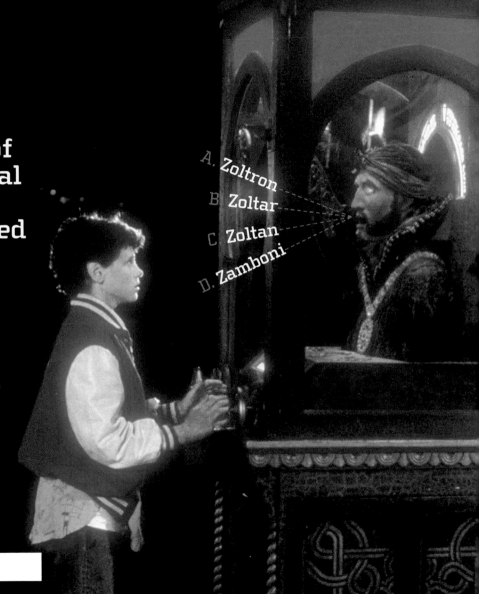

Answer:

1. Dennis Quaid

2. Fred Ward

# 26 Match the astronaut with the actor who portrayed him in 1983's The Right Stuff.

A. John Glenn    B. Alan Shepard
C. Gordon Cooper    D. Gus Grissom

3. Ed Harris

4. Scott Glenn

**27 BONUS**

Also in *The Right Stuff*, which astronaut's hatch blew, causing his space capsule to sink into the ocean?

**28** In the 1989 comedy *When Harry Met Sally...*, how does Sally (Meg Ryan) order ice cream for her pie and dressing for her salad?

**29** On a notorious 1989 cover of *TV Guide*, Oprah Winfrey's head was surreptitiously pasted onto another woman's body. Whose body was it?

A. Linda Evans
B. Angie Dickinson
C. Ann-Margret
D. Raquel Welch

**30** In 1989's *Major League*, the Cleveland Indians have to defeat what team in a one-game playoff to win the pennant?

**31** What is the name of the exclusive golf club in 1980's Caddyshack?

Answer:

80's
Classic TV Test Classic TV Test Classic TV Test

A few questions
about TV's alien
comedy ALF >>>

**32** What is ALF an acronym for?

**33** What's ALF's real name?

**34** What planet was he from?
A. Mallowmar
B. Melmac
C. Melanoid
D. Mars

**35** What's one of ALF's favorite catchphrases?
A. "Hasta la vista, baby."
B. "Ha, I kill me."
C. "Yo, Willie."
D. "No kidding?"

**36** TRUE OR FALSE? ALF returned in 2004 with a talk show airing on TV Land.

**37** What was the name of the Tanners' tasty-looking cat?

Answer:

## 38 How did reggae legend Bob Marley die (in 1981)?

■ A cancer        ■ B alcohol poisoning        ■ C car crash        ■ D heart attack

**39** Who told Senator Dan Quayle "You're no Jack Kennedy" during their televised vice-presidential debate in 1988?

**40** *The Shield* star Michael Chiklis portrayed a doomed real-life comic in a 1989 film. Name the comic and the movie.

**41** This famous line of dialogue comes from what 1987 comedy? "I'll meet you at the place near the thing where we went that time."

**42** In 1980's *The Idolmaker*, who played Vinnie Vacarri's (Ray Sharkey) last pop creation, Caesare?

A. Peter Scolari
B. Peter Gallagher
C. Deney Terrio
D. Tony Danza

**43** In the 1984 rockumentary *This Is Spiñal Tap*, how does David St. Hubbins (Michael McKean) say the band's original drummer died?

**44** BONUS
How did the second drummer die?

**45** In 1980's *Airplane!*, who is the onetime wholesome TV mom who delivers the line, "Oh, stewardess! I speak jive"?
A. Donna Reed
B. Florence Henderson
C. Shirley Jones
D. Barbara Billingsley

**46** Name the soap opera that makes Dorothy Michaels (Dustin Hoffman) a star in 1982's *Tootsie*.
A. *Southwest Hospital*
B. *Southwest General*
C. *Southwest Central*
D. *Southwest Passions*

# 47

## In 1987's Three Men and a Baby, who is the baby's real dad: Ted Danson, Tom Selleck, or Steve Guttenberg?

Answer:

# 48

Cosby kid **Lisa Bonet's** sexy role in this 1987 movie featuring **Robert De Niro** supposedly irked her wholesome TV dad, **Bill Cosby.**

Answer:

**49** What singer-songwriter composed UB40's huge 1988 number 1 single "Red Red Wine"?

---

**50** NAME THAT TUNE
This theme song, cowritten and sung by Gary Portnoy, accompanied what 1982 TV series? "Making your way in the world today takes everything you've got; Taking a break from all your worries sure would help a lot. Wouldn't you like to get away?"

---

**51** *Seinfeld*'s Michael Richards (aka Kramer) was a cast member on what late-night challenger to *Saturday Night Live*?

---

**52** What gift does Claire (Molly Ringwald) give to John (Judd Nelson) at the end of *The Breakfast Club*?

---

**53** On TV's Family Ties, name the Keaton neighbor who had a crush on Mallory (Justine Bateman).

## 54 What TV series spun off of Growing Pains?

Answer:

---

**55** Complete this last line of Spalding Gray's 1987 filmed monologue *Swimming to Cambodia*: "I suddenly thought I knew what it was that had killed ___."

A. Ernest Hemingway
B. Marilyn Monroe
C. Karl Marx
D. Sylvia Plath

---

**56** In which well-known Brat Pack flick does a frumpy Mare Winningham eat "the best peanut butter and jelly sandwich" she's ever had?

---

**57** Known for his role as anchorman Ted Baxter on *The Mary Tyler Moore Show*, Ted Knight returned to TV in the '80s with this sitcom about a cartoonist and his wife who share a house with their daughters.

---

**58** The opening scene of Woody Allen's *Broadway Danny Rose* takes place in what New York City landmark?

A. Metropolitan Museum of Art
B. Gershwin Theatre
C. Carnegie Deli
D. Lindy's

---

**59** In what city did the '80s TV cop drama *Hill Street Blues* take place?
A. Chicago
B. Philadelphia
C. New York
D. unknown

---

**60** Survivor's "Eye of the Tiger" was the theme to which *Rocky* film?

---

**61** More *Rocky*: When he famously runs up the steps in the original film, where is he?

---

**62** In 1985's *Back to the Future*, what brand of briefs does Marty McFly (Michael J. Fox) wear?

■ A. Jimi Hendrix

■ B. Bob Dylan

**63** In 1985's Desperately Seeking Susan, to which rock legend does Susan (Madonna) claim her jacket belonged?

■ C. Elvis

■ D. James Brown

# 64.

More Back to the Future: How many gigawatts of electricity will it take to spark the time machine and get Marty McFly home?

Answer:

A. 1 gigawatt

B. 1.21 gigawatts

C. 2 gigawatts

D. 100 gigawatts

**65** On TV's *Night Court*, Judge Harry Stone (Harry Anderson) had a fanatical devotion to what classic crooner?

A. Billy Eckstine
B. Mel Tormé
C. Tony Bennett
D. Sammy Davis Jr.

**66** Who played Pierce Brosnan's costar, private eye Laura Holt, on TV's *Remington Steele*?

**67** Complete this line from 1980's *The Elephant Man*: "I am not an animal. I am a __!"
A. mere curiosity
B. sideshow attraction
C. human being
D. desperate man

**68** In 1989's Bill & Ted's Excellent Adventure, Keanu Reeves (as Ted) quotes lyrics from which winsome song?

☐ A "Dream Weaver"     ☐ C "Every Breath You Take"
☐ B "Dust in the Wind"     ☐ D "Fire and Rain"

# Ultimate Fan Challenge:

Time to go back to the place "where everybody knows your name" and answer these ten brainteasers about *Cheers*.

**1.** The Cheers gang plays a joke on Frasier by taking him hunting for what imaginary creature?

_____

**2.** What's the name of the upscale restaurant above Cheers?

_____

**3.** What game show does Cliff appear on?

_____

**4.** Complete this memorable Norm Peterson entrance exchange: "What's shakin', Mr. Peterson?" "All four cheeks and ____."

_____

**5.** What was Carla and her husband Eddie LeBec's favorite song?

_____

**6.** How does Eddie LeBec—who was a Boston Bruins goalie—die?

_____

**7.** Here's another memorable Norm-ism: "How's it going, Mr. Peterson?" "It's a dog-eat-dog world, Woody, and I'm wearing ____."

_____

**8.** What is the lucky charm Sam lends his old baseball buddy who's on a losing streak?

_____

**9.** In the series finale, class-conscious Rebecca Howe married someone who does what for a living?
A. garbageman
B. electrician
C. plumber
D. pilot

_____

**10.** Which *Cheers* regular did NOT guest-star on the spin-off *Frasier*?
A. Woody Harrelson
B. Ted Danson
C. Shelley Long
D. Kirstie Alley

_____

**11** Match the nickname to the barfly.
☐A. Mayday  ☐B. Moonglow  ☐C. Backseat Becky  ☐D. The Hat

❶Norm  ❷Sam  ❸Harry the Con Man  ❹Rebecca Howe

# Cheers

## 69
**TRUE OR FALSE?** In 1981's *Raiders of the Lost Ark*, Indiana Jones never loses his hat.

Answer:

**70** In 1982's *The World According to Garp*, who played ex–football-player-turned-transsexual Roberta Muldoon?

**71** What famous comedian appeared in the video for Bobby McFerrin's 1988 novelty hit "Don't Worry Be Happy"?
A. Robin Williams
B. George Carlin
C. Henny Youngman
D. Ellen DeGeneres

**72** According to his diatribe in *Bull Durham*, whose writings did Crash Davis (Kevin Costner) think were "self-indulgent, overrated crap"?

**73** Who were the Traveling Wilburys?

**74** The Beach Boys' hit "Kokomo" came from what film's soundtrack?

**75** BONUS
According to the song, where is Kokomo located?

**76** At the Academy Awards in 1983, what film beat Steven Spielberg's *E.T. the Extra-Terrestrial* in the best picture race?
A. *Gandhi*
B. *Tootsie*
C. *The Verdict*
D. *Missing*

**77** What was Don Johnson's number 5 hit in 1986?
A. "Heartbeat"
B. "Heartbreaker"
C. "Heart Lights"
D. "Heart o' My Heart"

**78** Sylvester Stallone's 1987 action drama *Over the Top* centered on what sport?

**79** Who was the only performer to appear in both the London and Philadelphia Live Aid concerts?

**80** In his 1987 under-ground hit "Elvis Is Everywhere," who does Mojo Nixon claim is the "Anti-Elvis"?

A. Ellen DeGeneres

B. Oprah Winfrey

C. Rosie O'Donnell

D. Caroline Rhea

# 81

Which daytime talk-show host got her big break performing stand-up on an early episode of Star Search?

Answer:

1. Jerry O'Connell

2. Corey Feldman

**82** Match these stars of 1986's *Stand by Me* to their character name:

A. Chris Chambers    B. Gordie Lachance
C. Teddy Duchamp    D. Vern Tessio

3. Wil Wheaton

4. River Phoenix

**83** While we're on the subject of *Stand by Me*, who played Denny Lachance, Wil Wheaton's dead brother who is seen in flashbacks?

**84** In 1987, director Todd Haynes made a now-banned biopic—acted exclusively by Barbie and Ken dolls—about what singer's battle with anorexia?

**85** Who was David Letterman's first *Late Night* guest in 1982?
A. Chevy Chase
B. Gilda Radner
C. John Belushi
D. Bill Murray

**86** How did half-alien teen Evie (Maureen Flannigan) stop time on TV's *Out of This World*?
A. twitching her nose
B. swiveling her hips
C. clicking her heels together
D. touching her two index fingers together

**87** Who performs the horror rap at the end of Michael Jackson's megahit single "Thriller"?

Answer:

## 88 What were Westley's (Cary Elwes) words of love to Buttercup (Robin Wright Penn) in 1987's The Princess Bride?

Answer:

**92** Julian Sands played Helena Bonham Carter's main squeeze in 1985's *A Room With a View*, but who played her other paramour, Cecil?

**93** In which of these '80s movies does Meryl Streep NOT speak with a discernible accent?

A. *Silkwood*
B. *Plenty*
C. *Out of Africa*
D. *A Cry in the Dark*

**94** *The Simpsons* began as a recurring sketch on which Fox variety show?

**95** In the 1982 teen romp *Porky's*, what exactly was Porky's?

A. a strip club
B. a burger joint
C. a music hall
D. a brothel

**89** In what '80s comedy does the fictional mayor of New York City proclaim, "Being miserable and treating other people like dirt is every New Yorker's God-given right"?

A. *Ghostbusters II*
B. *Tootsie*
C. *Arthur*
D. *Arthur 2: On the Rocks*

**90** What Minnesota town did Rose (Betty White) grow up in on TV's *The Golden Girls*?

**91** Who is possessed by the "Gate Keeper" in 1984's *Ghostbusters*?

A. Venkman
B. Dana Barrett
C. Louis Tully
D. Gozer

# 96

What famous cowboy does John McClane (Bruce Willis) tell terrorists he's "partial to" in 1988's Die Hard?
Is it the Lone Ranger, Roy Rogers, or Gene Autry?

Answer:

1. Corey Haim

2. Corey Hart

3. Corey Feldman

# 97 Which famous Corey did what in the 1980s?

A. starred opposite River Phoenix in 1986's Stand by Me

B. had a hit single in 1984 with "Sunglasses at Night"

C. tried to save his brother from vampires in 1987's The Lost Boys

**98** Which famous celebrity is NOT mentioned in Madonna's hit single "Vogue"?

A. Greta Garbo

B. Marlon Brando

C. Fred Astaire

D. Humphrey Bogart

**99** In *The Cosby Show*, what was Rudy's (Keshia Knight Pulliam) favorite nickname for her friend Kenny?

**100** What symbol does Rocky Balboa (Sylvester Stallone) wear on his trunks for the climactic fight in 1985's *Rocky IV*?

**101** In 1981, whom did the cover of *Life* magazine proclaim as "America's Best Actress"?

A. Sally Field

B. Jane Fonda

C. Meryl Streep

D. Sissy Spacek

**102** What fellow Chicagoan appears in more than six movies—including *Say Anything* and *Serendipity*—with pal John Cusack?

**103** What Neil Diamond song was inspired by the film E.T. the Extra-Terrestrial?

Answer:

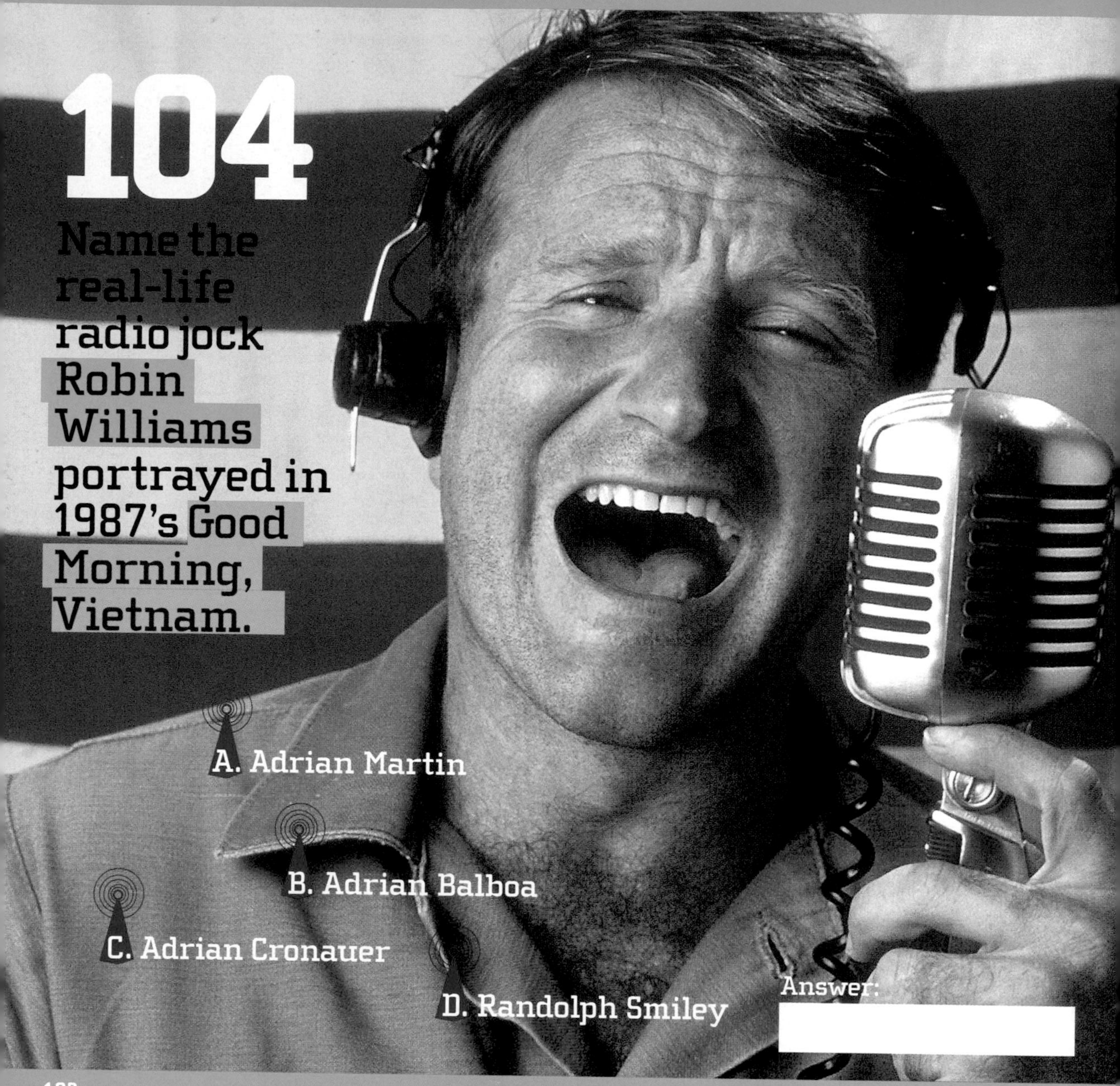

# 104

Name the real-life radio jock Robin Williams portrayed in 1987's Good Morning, Vietnam.

A. Adrian Martin

B. Adrian Balboa

C. Adrian Cronauer

D. Randolph Smiley

Answer:

A. Kajagoogoo

B. A Flock of Seagulls

# 105

## Match these '80s one-hit wonders to their hit.

1. "Take on Me"
2. "I Ran"
3. "Too Shy"
4. "Wild, Wild West"

C. The Escape Club

D. A-ha

## 106 What happens if you get a Mogwai wet in 1984's *Gremlins*?

Answer:

**107** TRUE OR FALSE? By inserting the words "penis breath" into the script, director Steven Spielberg earned 1982's *E.T. the Extra-Terrestrial* a PG rating.

**108** In 1986's *Top Gun*, which then unknown actress played the loving wife to Anthony Edwards's top flier, Goose?

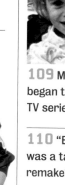

**109** Mary-Kate and Ashley Olsen began their careers on which '80s TV series?

**110** "Be afraid. Be very afraid" was a tagline to what 1986 sci-fi remake?

**111** The pivotal bet made by the aging Duke brothers (Ralph Bellamy and Don Ameche) in 1983's *Trading Places*—whether a petty criminal could be made into a successful businessman—was for how much money?

A. $1 million
B. $10,000
C. $1
D. $100

**112** Film critic Pauline Kael wrote, "When the discreet classical music starts...you know it's going to reek of quality." Which 1980 best picture nominee was she reviewing?
A. *Ordinary People*
B. *Raging Bull*
C. *Tess*
D. *The Elephant Man*

**113** What R&B singer extols the benefits of "dancing on the ceiling"?

**114** Where did Jason Voorhees go on his rampage in 1980's *Friday the 13th*?

# 115

The song "Call Me," by Blondie, became a number 1 hit after it was featured in what 1980 movie?

Answer:

# 116

In Beverly Hills Cop, what fruit does Axel Foley (Eddie Murphy) use to disable a police car?

☐ A. Grapes

☐ B. Kiwi

☐ C. Peach

☐ D. Banana

**117** Complete this line from 1988's *Who Framed Roger Rabbit*: "I'm not bad, ___."

**118 BONUS**
Who said it?

**119** Who turned down Steven Spielberg's offer to appear as blues singer Shug Avery in his 1985 film version of *The Color Purple*?
A. Diana Ross
B. Whitney Houston
C. Valerie Simpson
D. Tina Turner

**120** What cartoon strong man was made into a live-action big-screen hero alongside Courteney Cox in 1987?
A. He-Man
B. the Incredible Hulk
C. Hercules
D. Popeye

**121** Who were the robot sidekicks built by Joel the janitor on *Mystery Science Theater 3000*?

**122** On TV's The A-Team, Mr. T's B. A. Baracus had one phobia. Name it.

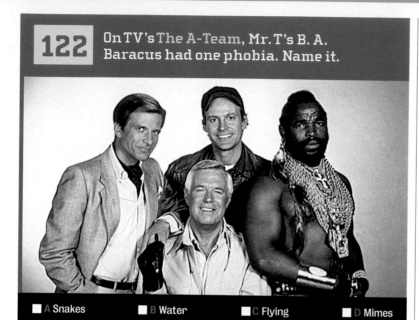

☐ A Snakes ☐ B Water ☐ C Flying ☐ D Mimes

**127** Bill Murray and Harold Ramis appeared together in what three '80s-era films directed by Ivan Reitman?

**128** Before Eddie Murphy was cast, who was originally slated to play Axel Foley in 1984's *Beverly Hills Cop*?
A. Richard Pryor
B. Arnold Schwarzenegger
C. Martin Lawrence
D. Sylvester Stallone

**123** What was the name of Nirvana's first single?

**124** Name the cartoonist who is responsible for Bill the Cat and Opus in *Bloom County*.
A. Gary Trudeau
B. Irwin Hasen
C. Berkeley Breathed
D. Chic Young

**125** According to the sequel to *2001: A Space Odyssey*, what happens in 2010?

**126** Who was the most frequent female guest host of *The Tonight Show*?

**129** What '80s-era TV medical drama had a twist ending that indicated the whole series was just a young child's dream?

**130** Which original *Love Boat* star went on to serve as a congressman?
A. Ted Lange
B. Bernie Kopell
C. Fred Grandy
D. Gavin MacLeod

**131** Name the author who chronicled his tale of abduction by aliens in the 1987 best seller *Communion*.

# 132

Which big-name author wrote the novel The Running Man (which became an Arnold Schwarzenegger movie) under the nom de plume Richard Bachman?

A. John Grisham

B. Tom Wolfe

C. Stephen King

D. Michael Crichton

Answer:

# The 1990s

Friends  Up Close & Personal  The Wonder Years  The Truman Show  Leonardo
DiCaprio  **Mr. Show**  Single White Female  Get Shorty  The Usual Suspects
Home Improvement  A League of Their Own  LeAnn Rimes  Apollo 13  NYPD Blue
The Bodyguard  Nirvana  Misery  Twister  Public Enemy  **Seinfeld**  Tin Cup
L.A. Confidential  Melrose Place  Jay Leno  Gloria Estefan  Drew Carey  R.E.M.
Murphy Brown  The Simpsons  Baywatch  Office Space  Des'ree  Everybody
Loves Raymond  **American Beauty**  The Shawshank Redemption
Garth Brooks  Jurassic Park  Austin Powers  The Commitments  Scent of a
Woman  The Silence of the Lambs  Forrest Gump  The Spice Girls  Buffy the
Vampire Slayer  Saving Private Ryan  Titanic  Felicity  Clueless  The Green Mile
Dawson's Creek  Wayne's World  **Independence Day**  Magnolia
That Thing You Do!  Eyes Wide Shut  Frasier City Slickers  Fargo  Bob Roberts

**1** Fred Savage played the part of young Kevin Arnold on *The Wonder Years*, but who provided the voice of the adult Kevin?

Answer:

**2** The Robert Redford–Michelle Pfeiffer TV news romance *Up Close & Personal* was based on what real-life reporter's life?

**3** What is the name of the boat that Truman Burbank (Jim Carrey) uses to escape his insulated world in 1998's *The Truman Show*?
A. *Mayflower*
B. *Nostromo*
C. *Santa Maria*
D. *Monkey Business*

**4** What 1990s film was the first to win best director, best actor, and the Palme d'Or (for best film) at the Cannes Film Festival?
A. *Barton Fink* (1991)
B. *Pulp Fiction* (1994)
C. *Shine* (1996)
D. *The Straight Story* (1999)

**5** In the 1992 thriller *Single White Female*, with what weapon does Hedy (Jennifer Jason Leigh) kill Sam (Steven Weber)?

**6** What 1993 movie earned Leonardo DiCaprio his first Academy Award nomination?

**7** Who was the captain of the Love Boat when it relaunched in 1998 as *The Love Boat: The Next Wave*?

**8** In 1995's *Get Shorty*, what is the title of Martin Weir's (Danny DeVito) autobiography?

**9** More on *Get Shorty*: In the end, who directs Chili Palmer's movie?

**10** What ethnicity was the mysterious Keyser Söze in 1995's *The Usual Suspects*?
A. Iranian
B. Turkish
C. Greek
D. Arab

**11** What was the name of Tim Taylor's (Tim Allen) wise neighbor on TV's *Home Improvement*?

A. Max Weinberg

B. Kevin Eubanks

C. Paul Shaffer

# 12 Match the band leader to their late-night gig:

1. The Late Show with
**David Letterman**

2. The Tonight Show with
**Jay Leno**

3. Late Night with
**Conan O'Brien**

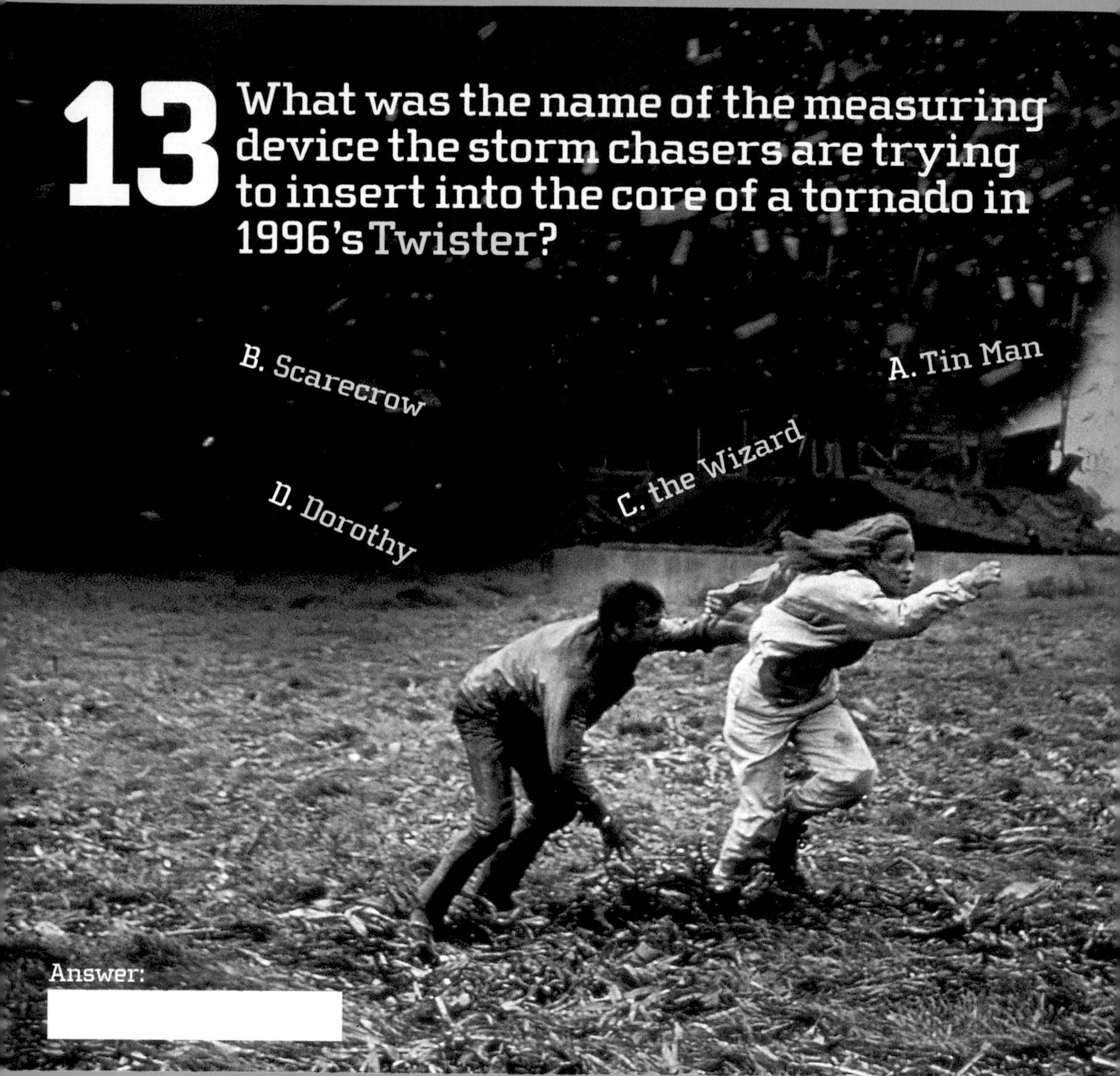

# 13

What was the name of the measuring device the storm chasers are trying to insert into the core of a tornado in 1996's Twister?

A. Tin Man

B. Scarecrow

C. the Wizard

D. Dorothy

Answer:

**14** In 1994's *The Adventures of Priscilla Queen of the Desert*, starring Terence Stamp, who is Priscilla?

**15** Before he became a late-night host, Conan O'Brien was a staff writer for which late-night comedy show?

**16** In 1997, who did Kevin Costner claim was considering starring opposite him in a sequel to the 1992 hit *The Bodyguard*?

A. Sarah Ferguson
B. Princess Diana
C. Princess Caroline
D. Barbra Streisand

**17** LeAnn Rimes's hit "Blue" was originally written for which country legend to sing?

**18** David Fincher directed the 1995 Brad Pitt thriller Se7en. What other '90s film did he direct also starring Pitt?

Answer:

**19** What potential illness kept Ken Mattingly (Gary Sinise) from being part of the Apollo 13 crew in the 1995 Ron Howard film?

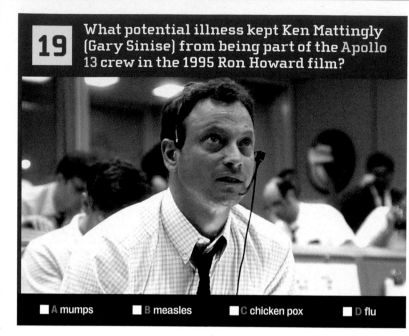

☐ A mumps    ☐ B measles    ☐ C chicken pox    ☐ D flu

**20** Controversy erupted in 1994 when *Time* magazine was accused of doing what to the famous mug shot of O. J. Simpson that ran on its cover?

**21** In the 1990 film *Misery*, Annie Wilkes (Kathy Bates) breaks Paul Sheldon's (James Caan) legs with a sledgehammer in order to prevent him from gaining mobility. How is this different from what happens in Stephen King's novel?

**22** Who did rappers Public Enemy say was "a hero to most/But he never meant shit to me"?

A. Nelson Mandela
B. Martin Luther King Jr.
C. Desmond Tutu
D. Elvis Presley

**23** *These Friends of Mine* was the original title of what groundbreaking TV sitcom?

**24** In 1997's *L.A. Confidential*, Kim Basinger was supposed to emulate which '40s screen starlet?

**25** On *Melrose Place*, Michael Mancini (Thomas Calabro) was NOT married to

A. Jane
B. Sydney
C. Amanda
D. Kimberly

**26** To which film-star guest did *The Tonight Show*'s Jay Leno say, "What the hell were you thinking?"

**27** What movie was ranked number 1 of the twentieth century on the British Film Institute's top 100?
A. *Lawrence of Arabia*
B. *Brief Encounter*
C. *The Third Man*
D. *Chariots of Fire*

**28** What American actor died on the same day, Halloween 1993, as Italian filmmaking legend Federico Fellini?

# 29

Who substituted for a reportedly ailing Luciano Pavarotti to sing "Nessun dorma" at the 1998 Grammy Awards?

A. Whitney Houston

B. Plácido Domingo

C. Aretha Franklin

D. Jewel

# 30

What is the name of the fast-food chain that Lester Burnham (Kevin Spacey) takes a job at in 1999's Oscar-winning American Beauty?

**A.** Mr. Smiley's    **B.** Magic Wanda    **C.** King Benny's    **D.** Happy Face

**31** In the short-lived 1999 sci-fi series *Now and Again*, Eric Close played the genetically improved Michael Wiseman. What famous actor played the original Wiseman—before his body was hit by an oncoming subway train?

**32** What's the name of the TV news-magazine where Murphy Brown worked?

**33** Who inspired R.E.M.'s hit "Man on the Moon"?

**34** On TV's *The Drew Carey Show*, what is Buzz Beer?

**35** TRUE OR FALSE? You can find a life-size replica of *The Simpsons*' multicolored four-bedroom home in Henderson, Nevada.

**36** In what state did singer Gloria Estefan have her near-fatal bus accident in 1990?
A. Florida
B. California
C. Washington
D. Pennsylvania

**37** Which Kiss tune did Garth Brooks record on a 1994 tribute album?

A "Beth"     B "Hard Luck Woman"     C "Christine Sixteen"     D "Love Gun"

**38** What company does Peter Gibbons (Ron Livingston) work for in Mike Judge's 1999 comedy Office Space?

■ A Initech        ■ B Intel        ■ C TechTel        ■ D Boeing

**39** The design for what legendary figure's postage stamp was decided by a nationwide vote in 1992, with the more youthful version winning over the older-looking one?

**40** What's the fictitious identity Andy Dufresne (Tim Robbins) creates to skip town with the embezzled prison money in The Shawshank Redemption?
A. Randall Smith
B. Randall Stephens
C. Randall George
D. Thurston Randall

**41** In 1992's Scent of a Woman, how did Lieutenant Colonel Frank Slade (Al Pacino) go blind?

A. on the battlefield
B. in a plane crash
C. a drinking/grenade game
D. a degenerative disease

**42** Which future Baywatch star also appeared on Charles in Charge?

**43** Drew Barrymore was the teenage seductress in 1992's Poison Ivy. What TV actress charmed audiences playing the seductress role in the '96 sequel?

**44** Jurassic Park was the highest-grossing film of all time, until what 1997 juggernaut came along and knocked it to second place?

**45** Who plays the president of the United States in 1999's Austin Powers: The Spy Who Shagged Me?
A. Michael York
B. Tim Robbins
C. Rob Lowe
D. Tom Cruise

**46** In 1991's The Silence of the Lambs, Clarice (Jodie Foster) finds the cocoon of what kind of moth in the throat of a murder victim?

1. Madonna

2. Lori Petty

# 47

## Match the actress with the field position she played in 1992's A League of Their Own

- ☐ A. Center Field
- ☐ C. Catcher
- ☐ B. Pitcher
- ☐ D. Third Base

3. Geena Davis

4. Rosie O'Donnell

90's

Test Classic TV Test Classic TV Test Classic TV

# The series ran for nine seasons—
## see if you know these **Seinfeld** facts >>>

**BONUS!**
**54** According to the series finale of
*Seinfeld*, who really won "The Contest"?

**48** Yes, the name sounded like a female body part—but it wasn't Mulva. What was Jerry's date's actual name?

**49** What's the name George is saving for his future baby that friends later steal?

**50** Put the *Seinfeld* characters in the order in which they dropped out of "The Contest."

**51** What killed George's fiancée, Susan?

**52** What is the geometric name that Kramer would give his child, if he had one?

A. Triangle
B. Isosceles
C. Radius
D. Parallelogram

**53** Which actress played which of Jerry's girlfriends on *Seinfeld*?

1. Kristin Davis    2. Jane Leeves

☐ A. the one with the possible breast implants

☐ B. the one with the toothbrush that fell in the toilet

☐ C. the virgin

☐ D. the one who likes cereal and Superman

3. Teri Hatcher    4. Janeane Garofalo

## 55 What famous rock critic did Philip Seymour Hoffman portray in Almost Famous?

Answer:

**56** In the 1994 Tom Hanks block-buster *Forrest Gump*, what up-and-coming young actor played Forrest's son?

**57** Which celebrity did NOT have a cameo appearance in 1997's *Spice World*?
A. Elton John
B. Phil Collins
C. Elvis Costello
D. Bob Geldof

**58** In 1998's *Saving Private Ryan*, how many of the titular soldier's brothers were killed?
A. three
B. four
C. two
D. one

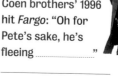

**59** Complete this line of dialogue from the Coen brothers' 1996 hit *Fargo*: "Oh for Pete's sake, he's fleeing ............................ "

# 60

What Chris Isaak song was memorably featured in Stanley Kubrick's 1999 film *Eyes Wide Shut*?

A. "Don't Make Me Dream About You"

B. "Baby Did a Bad Bad Thing"

C. "Wicked Game"

D. "Walk Slow"

Answer:

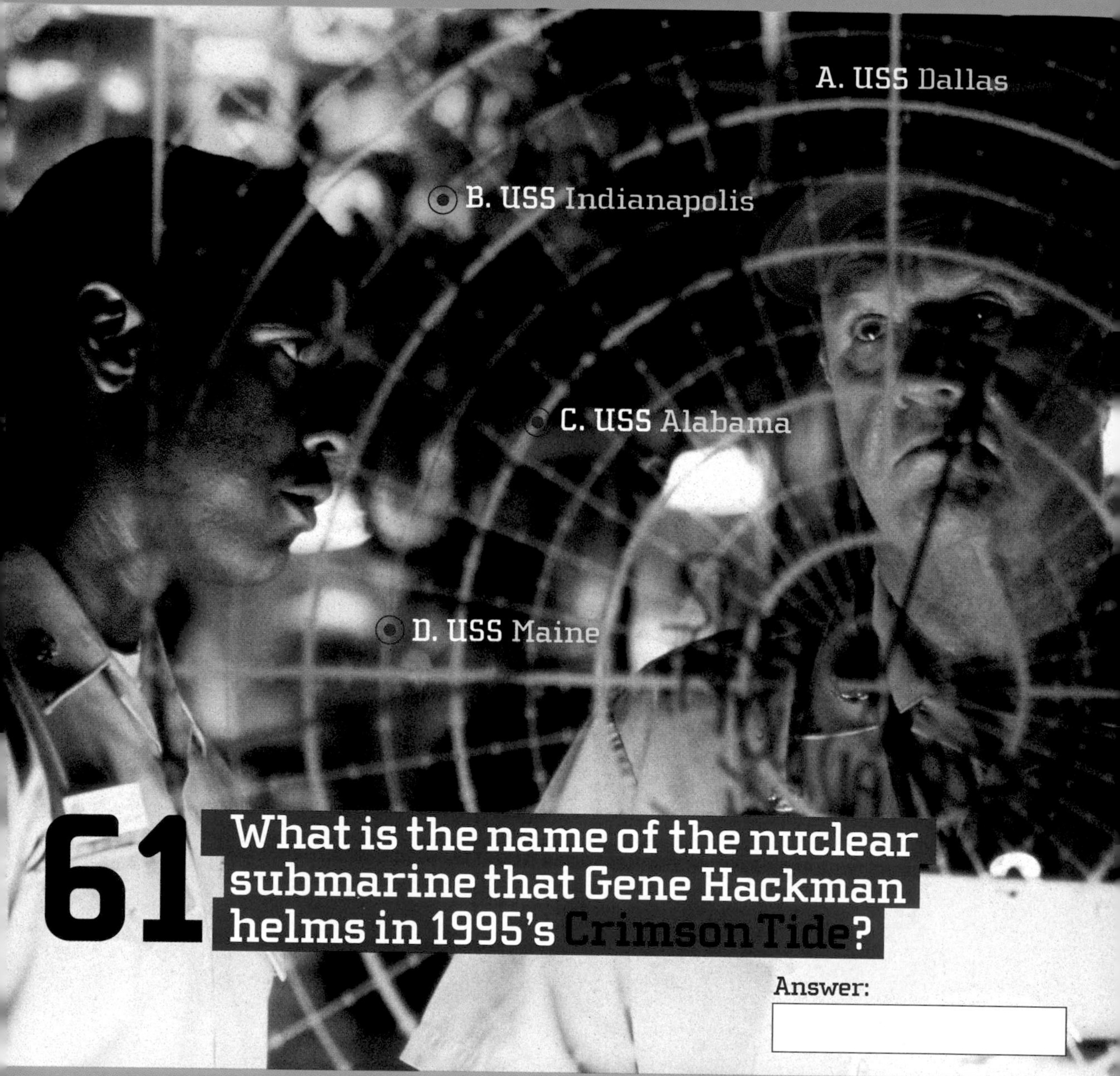

A. USS Dallas

◉ B. USS Indianapolis

C. USS Alabama

◉ D. USS Maine

# 61

What is the name of the nuclear submarine that Gene Hackman helms in 1995's Crimson Tide?

Answer:

**62** Chris Farley famously played a Chippendales dancer on a '90s-era episode of *Saturday Night Live* alongside what movie star?

**63** Before she won an Oscar for *Boys Don't Cry*, Hilary Swank guest-starred as a single mother on what popular '90s TV series?

**64** During the Persian Gulf War, which NBC news reporter became known as the "Scud Stud"?

**65** In 1997's *Volcano*, lava spills onto the streets of Los Angeles from what popular tourist sight?
A. the Ivy
B. La Brea Tar Pits
C. People's Park
D. Jerry's Famous Deli

**66** In 1997's *Titanic*, who actually did the drawings that appear in Jack's (Leonardo DiCaprio) sketchbook, including the one of Rose wearing the necklace?

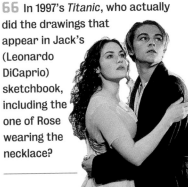

**67** According to the 1995 film **Clueless**, what does it mean to be a total Baldwin?

**Answer:**

**68** Which baseball team did George Clooney once try out for?
A. Cincinnati Reds
B. Chicago Cubs
C. Los Angeles Dodgers
D. Philadelphia Phillies

**69** Name the Fox sitcom starring *Sideways*'s Thomas Haden Church and *Will & Grace*'s Debra Messing as two people who got married so she could have an apartment and he could look good to his employer.

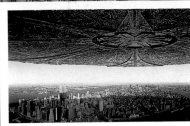

**70** In 1996's doomsday drama *Independence Day*, what finally leads to the demise of the attacking aliens?
A. nuclear bomb
B. flu virus
C. computer virus
D. water

**71** In the Highlander TV series, what is the only way to kill an immortal?

Answer:

**72** What is the name of Eduard Delacroix's (Michael Jeter) pet death row mouse in 1999's *The Green Mile*?

**73** What 1991 film, directed by Sean Penn, was inspired by the Bruce Springsteen song "Highway Patrolman"?

**74** To which heavy metal star do Wayne and Garth (Mike Myers and Dana Carvey) confess "We're not worthy" in 1992's *Wayne's World*?
A. Alice Cooper
B. Ozzy Osbourne
C. Axl Rose
D. Tommy Lee

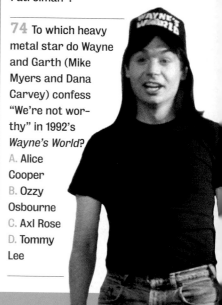

A. Alanis Morissette

B. Tori Amos

C. Jewel

D. Joan Osborne

# 75 Match the hit single to the '90s songstress

- ☐ 1. "I Don't Want to Wait"
- ☐ 2. "One of Us"
- ☐ 3. "You Oughta Know"
- ☐ 4. "God"
- ☐ 5. "Who Will Save Your Soul"

E. Paula Cole

# 76

## Name the hosts of the '90s-era series Mr. Show

Answer:

**77** In 1996, who anonymously purchased Clark Gable's best actor Oscar for 1934's *It Happened One Night* at a Christie's auction for more than $600,000, and promptly returned it to the academy?

A. Harvey Weinstein
B. Martin Scorsese
C. Steven Spielberg
D. Clint Eastwood

**78** Before embarking on a solo career in the mid–1990s, Natalie Merchant fronted what popular folk-rock band?

**79** In a 1993 production of David Mamet's *Oleanna* in Sydney, Australia, what then–unknown actress played opposite Geoffrey Rush in the two-person play?

A. Charlize Theron
B. Naomi Watts
C. Rachel Griffiths
D. Cate Blanchett

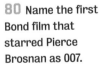

**80** Name the first Bond film that starred Pierce Brosnan as 007.

**81** On *Frasier*, where in England is live-in help Daphne Moon (Jane Leeves) from?

**82** Which Fox network sketch-comedy show gave Jim Carrey his "big break"?

Answer:

**83** More about *Frasier*: What's the name of the coffee shop that Frasier and Niles frequent?

A. Café Nirvana
B. Café Navidad
C. Café Amarosa
D. Café Nervosa

**84** What was the title of the 1990 sequel to *Chinatown*?

**85** Which country legend sang on the KLF's "Justified & Ancient"?

**86** Denzel Washington played a Persian Gulf War vet in the recent *Manchurian Candidate*. He also played one in what '90s-era military drama starring Meg Ryan?

# Ultimate Fan Challenge:

They were there for you, and you happily returned the favor. So we're certain you can recall these ten things about *Friends*.

**1** What disease did Joey inadvertently become poster boy for?

**2** Which popular song did Marcel, Ross's monkey, really seem to enjoy?
A. "Jungle Boogie"
B. "The Lion Sleeps Tonight"
C. "Jungle Love"
D. "Can You Feel the Love Tonight?"

**3** Which famous actress on Ross's "Freebie List" (five stars he was allowed to sleep with without jeopardizing his relationship with Rachel) shows up in Central Park?

**4** Phoebe's relationship with scientist David (Hank Azaria) doesn't last because he ended up moving to which European city?
A. Prague
B. Antwerp
C. Minsk
D. Paris

**5** Which song does Rachel sing to overcome her fears at ex-fiancé Barry's wedding to her best friend Mindy?

**6** Where did Ross and Rachel first have sex?

**7** More *Friends* geography. In order to stop seeing Janice, where did Chandler tell her his job was transferring him?

**8** What was Joey's character's name on *Days of Our Lives*?

**9** According to Phoebe, it was "what evil must taste like," but what was the name of the disgusting chocolate substitute Monica was hired to make recipes with?

**10** Who sang the *Friends* theme song?

# Friends

# 87

**What was Roy McAvoy's (Kevin Costner) score on the last hole of 1996's Tin Cup?**

A. 11

B. 12

C. 13

D. 14

Answer:

**88** What is the date of Judgment Day in 1991's *Terminator 2: Judgment Day*?

A. August 24, 1997
B. August 29, 1997
C. August 4, 1997
D. July 4, 1997

**89** What musical instrument did Claudia Salinger (Lacey Chabert) play on TV's *Party of Five*?

A. violin
B. piano
C. oboe
D. trumpet

**90** Name the 1994 Des'ree single that spent forty-four weeks on the *Billboard* charts.

**91** In the 1992 satire, Tim Robbins's slimy folk singer *Bob Roberts* runs for senator in what state?

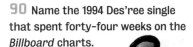

A. New York
B. New Jersey
C. Pennsylvania
D. Delaware

**92** On *Beverly Hills, 90210*, what fraternity does Steve (Ian Ziering) join?

☐ A KEG   ☐ B OMEGA   ☐ C DELTA   ☐ D TAP

## 93
In *Dawson's Creek*, what was the name of Pacey's (Joshua Jackson) boat?

**Answer:**

**98** Name the 1999 film that features Tim Robbins and Joan Cusack as a suburban couple who are suspected of being terrorists.

**99** What 1990s best picture Oscar winner was the first since 1966 to win the top prize without its screenplay being nominated?

**100** What supermodel graced the premiere cover of *George* magazine dressed as the Father of Our Country?

**101** On *Everybody Loves Raymond*, Robert (Brad Garrett) names his dog after which former New York Met?

**102** More on *Raymond*: What's Debra's (Patricia Heaton) most common recipe?

**94** Which one of these '90s films was the first completely computer-generated feature?
A. *The Lion King*
B. *Toy Story*
C. *A Bug's Life*
D. *Antz*

**95** What movie musical was a big-screen success for Madonna in 1996?

**96** Which now grown-up child TV star joined the cast of *NYPD Blue* in 1998?

**97** What French filmmaker made a crossover to Hollywood when he directed 1997's *Alien: Resurrection*?

A. Luc Besson
B. Jean-Jacques Annaud
C. Jean-Pierre Jeunet
D. Olivier Assayas

# 103

Counter-culture guru Timothy Leary is the godfather of which Reality Bites star?

A: Winona Ryder

B. Ethan Hawke

C. Janeane Garofalo

D. Ben Stiller

Answer:

# 104

In 1993's
Jurassic Park,
what's the
species of dino
that stalks
Lex and Tim
(Ariana
Richards,
Joseph
Mazzello) in
the kitchen?

Answer:

**105** In 1997's *My Best Friend's Wedding*, what kind of writer is Julianne Potter (Julia Roberts)?

**106** Which product was advertised by an infomercial that promised "a lean mean fat-reducing grilling machine"?

A. Ab-Away

B. Bowflex

C. Scunci Steamer

D. George Foreman Grill

**107** What actress has a cameo appearance as a judge in the last scene of 1998's *A Civil Action*, starring John Travolta?

A. Meryl Streep

B. Kathy Bates

C. Olivia Newton-John

D. Holly Hunter

**108** Soap star Susan Lucci finally won a Daytime Emmy in 1999 after having been nominated how many times before?

■ A nine    ■ B twelve    ■ C eighteen    ■ D twenty

# 109

**Thomas Crown (Pierce Brosnan again) steals a painting by what famous artist in the 1999 version of The Thomas Crown Affair?**

**A. Renoir**  **B. Rembrandt**  **C. Manet**  **D. Monet**

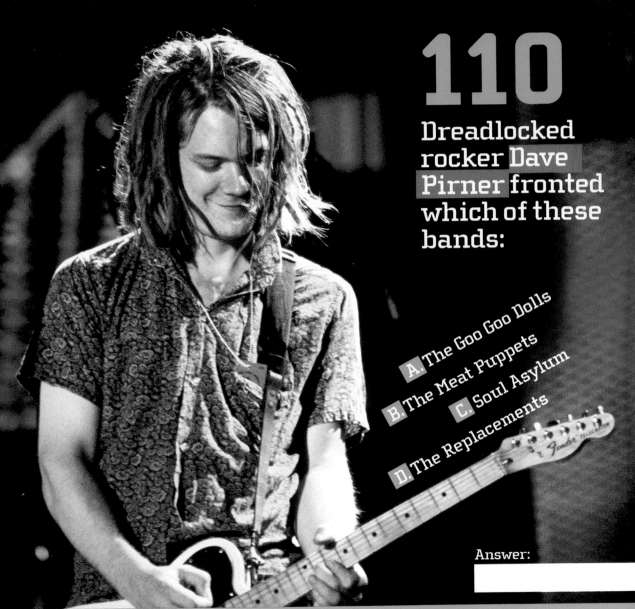

# 110

Dreadlocked rocker Dave Pirner fronted which of these bands:

A. The Goo Goo Dolls

B. The Meat Puppets

C. Soul Asylum

D. The Replacements

Answer:

## 111 Where were the Wonders from in 1996's *That Thing You Do!*?

■ A Philadelphia, PA    ■ B Erie, PA    ■ C Reading, PA    ■ D West Chester, PA

**112** Another FAQ about *That Thing You Do!* What's the original spelling of the band's name?

**113** Sean Connery costarred with Wesley Snipes in which big-screen adaptation of a Michael Crichton novel?

**114** What famous filmmaker portrays Vincent van Gogh in a scene at the end of 1990's *Akira Kurosawa's Dreams*?
A. Roman Polanski
B. Francis Ford Coppola
C. Stanley Kubrick
D. Martin Scorsese

**115** What profession did Daniel Day-Lewis consider—as an alternate to acting—at the end of 1998?

**116** The songs of what female musician were featured extensively on the soundtrack to 1999's ensemble movie *Magnolia*?

A. k.d. lang
B. Tracy Chapman
C. Aimee Mann
D. Fiona Apple

**117** Which of these '90s-era films did NOT feature Kris Kristofferson?
A. *Lone Star*
B. *Wag the Dog*
C. *Blade*
D. *Payback*

**118** What does the J stand for in Homer J. Simpson?

A. John
B. Jonas
C. Joshua
D. Jay

**119** Canadian or not? Pick the '90s-era pop singer who does NOT hail from the north.
A. Celine Dion
B. k.d. lang
C. Natalie Imbruglia
D. Sarah McLachlan

**120** In the series Buffy the Vampire Slayer, what was the name of Buffy's stake?

Answer:

# 121

Butch Vig, who produced Nirvana's Nevermind, is drummer for what band.ɔ

Answer:

**122** Which famous soul singer said he would come jam with *The Commitments* in the 1991 film?

**123** In 1992, what did *City Slickers* star Jack Palance do at the Academy Awards after he was named best supporting actor?

**124** Which NBA star did NOT appear in the 1996 film *Space Jam*?
A. Michael Jordan
B. Charles Barkley
C. Larry Bird
D. Scottie Pippen

**125** On *Felicity*, what condiment did Ben's roommate Sean invent?

**126** Speaking of *Felicity*, which real-life New York City coffee shop did Keri Russell work at on the WB series?

☐ A Dean & DeLuca    ☐ B Starbucks    ☐ C Java Joe's    ☐ D Timothy's

147

# The 2000s

The Lord of the Rings **Sideways** Anchorman Mulholland Dr. Ocean's Eleven The West Wing Spider-Man Good Charlotte My Big Fat Greek Wedding Lost in Translation Shallow Hal Sky Captain and the World of Tomorrow Norah Jones **Cast Away** Lost O Brother, Where Art Thou? Alias Everwood Eternal Sunshine of the Spotless Mind Holes The Killers Scrubs Miracle 'N Sync Shadow of the Vampire **Sex and the City** Million Dollar Baby Master and Commander Punch-Drunk Love CSI The Sopranos Survivor School of Rock Joe Millionaire The Ring Desperate Housewives Lindsay Lohan Hilary Duff **Janet Jackson** Goldmember Friday Night Lights Ken Jennings on Jeopardy! Garden State Numb3rs Julia Roberts Madonna LL Cool J Daniel Day-Lewis Melissa Etheridge Drew Barrymore Six Feet Under Revenge of the Sith The O.C. **Saturday Night Live**

**1** What name did **Madonna** adopt after she began practicing Kabbalah?

Answer:

**6** What is the name of the club that the characters visit in David Lynch's 2001 fantasia *Mulholland Dr.*? (It is also the last word spoken in the film.)
A. Finito
B. Fidelio
C. Silencio
D. Serenity

**2** In March 2000, whom did *Forbes* magazine name as the most powerful celebrity in the world?
A. Tom Cruise
B. Julia Roberts
C. Oprah Winfrey
D. Nicole Kidman

**3** What was the name of *The X-Files*'s 2001 spinoff?

**4** What actor played Polonius to Ethan Hawke's Hamlet in the 2000 adaptation of Shakespeare's play?

**5** What was Ron Burgundy's (Will Ferrell) sign-off at the end of each newscast in 2004's *Anchorman: The Legend of Ron Burgundy*?

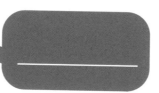

**7** Simon & Garfunkel invited which rock-and-roll founders to sing with them on their 2004 tour?

**8** Fill in this line from 2001's *Ocean's Eleven*: "——— called. He wants your shirt back." Was it Ted Nugent, Steven Tyler, or Alice Cooper?

# 9 What Saturday Night Live cast member was once a member of theater's Blue Man Group?

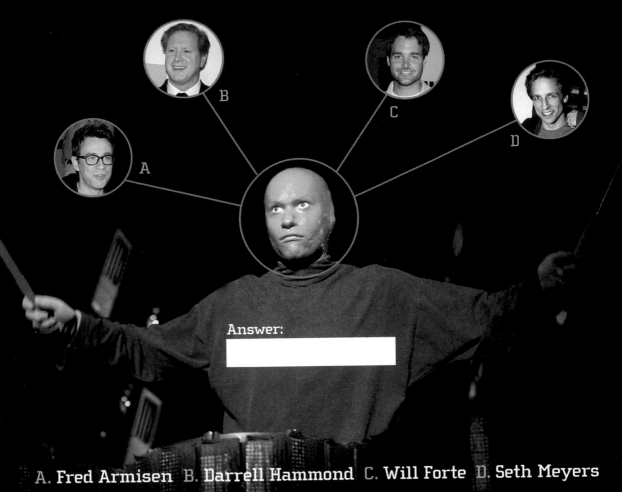

B

C

D

A

Answer:

A. Fred Armisen  B. Darrell Hammond  C. Will Forte  D. Seth Meyers

# 10

## Where does Good Charlotte hail from?

A. Waldorf, Maryland

B. Charlotte, North Carolina

C. Charlottesville, Virginia

D. Springfield, Ohio

Answer:

**11** On TV's *The West Wing*, what did Leo McGarry (John Spencer) write on a napkin to persuade Jed (Martin Sheen) to run for president?

**12** Another *West Wing* FAQ: Martin Sheen's president was formerly a governor from which U.S. state?

A. New York
B. Maine
C. New Hampshire
D. Massachusetts

**13** Who played Austin Powers's father, Nigel, in 2002's *Goldmember*?

**14** What is the name of the professional wrestler whom Peter Parker (Tobey Maguire) defeats in 2000's *Spider-Man*?

A Bone Cruncher   B Bonesaw   C Bone Breaker   D The Killer

**15** On TV's *Lost*, what did Hurley do with "the numbers" that eventually brought him to Australia?

Answer:

**16** Who is Jeffrey Atkins?
A. Jay-Z
B. LL Cool J
C. Ja Rule
D. Jam Master Jay

**17** What do Teri Polo, Valerie Bertinelli, Anthony Anderson, and Judge Reinhold have in common?
A. They all worked at the Pasadena Playhouse.
B. They were all born in Delaware.
C. They all attended UCLA.
D. They all own a piece of a baseball team.

**18** What famous musician is Norah Jones's father?

A. George Harrison
B. Ravi Shankar
C. Philip Glass
D. Tom Scott

**19** Whose cameo in 2004's *Sky Captain and the World of Tomorrow* occurred fifteen years after his death?

**20** In 2004's *Sideways*, which wine does Paul Giamatti's character Miles detest?

**21** How many times did champion Ken Jennings win on *Jeopardy!*?

A. 38
B. 56
C. 74
D. 112

**22** More about Jennings: What was the question to the answer that finally stumped him?

**23** Which TV pundit did Senator Zell Miller challenge to a duel?
A. Tucker Carlson
B. Tim Russert
C. Jack Germond
D. Chris Matthews

Before Mischa Barton shared a romantic beachfront lip-lock with Olivia Wilde on The O.C., she had a same-sex kiss with actress Evan Rachel Wood on this drama featuring Sela Ward.

Answer:

Sarah Jessica Parker starred as a fashion-conscious newspaper columnist on **Sex and the City.**
Here's a quiz on the breakthrough series >>>

**25** What did Stanford call a runway-fallen Carrie (Parker) when she got stepped over by supermodel Heidi Klum?

**26** What did Berger (Ron Livingston) use to break up with Carrie?

**27** How does Charlotte (Kristin Davis) meet Trey MacDougal (Kyle MacLachlan), whom she eventually marries?

**28** Which pop singer smooched with Carrie over a game of spin the bottle?
A. Beyoncé
B. Alanis Morissette
C. Sarah McLachlan
D. Madonna

**29** In the show finale, what do we discover is Mr. Big's real name?

**30** Who helps Aidan (John Corbett) pick out the engagement ring that Carrie hates?

Answer:

# 31

In 2003's School of Rock, what uptight private prep school does Dewey Finn's (Jack Black) fledgling rock band attend?

A. Dalton

B. Horace Mann

C. Horace Green

D. Welton Academy

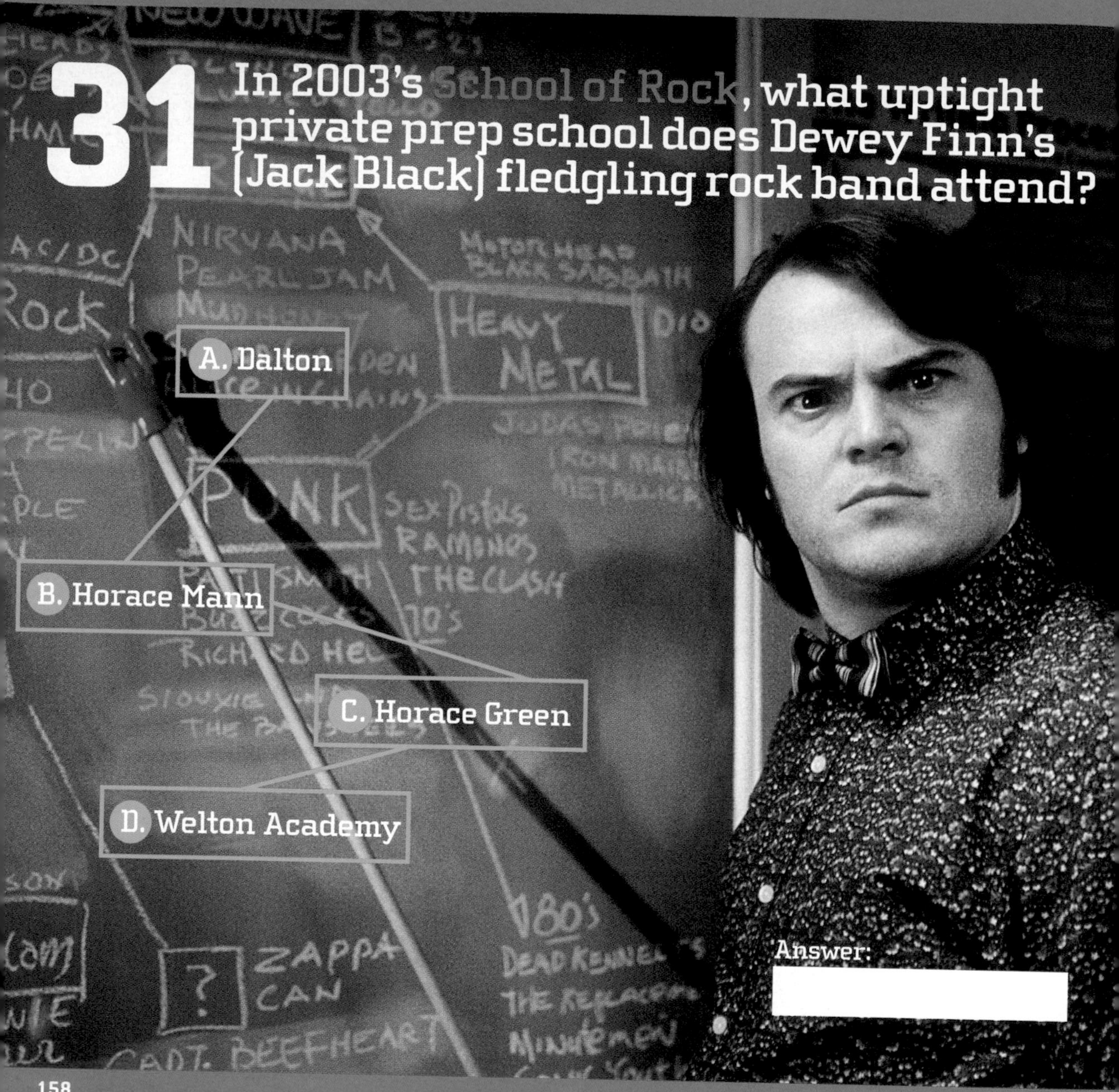

Answer:

**32** What are the films produced in the 2000s that make up director Steven Spielberg's unofficial "running man" trilogy?

**33** At the 2005 Oscar ceremony, what supporting actress winner thanked her director by saying, "I hope my son will marry your daughter"?

**34** Name the twins born to Julia Roberts in 2004.

**35** What is the name of the odor-killing miracle product in *Holes*?

**36** Which *Sopranos* "family guy" likes to imitate Al Pacino in *The Godfather: Part III*, "Just when I thought I was out, they pull me back in"?

A. Silvio
B. Paulie
C. Pussy
D. Tony

**37** In what city do Bill Murray and Scarlett Johansson meet in 2003's Lost in Translation?

Answer:

**38** What product does the small business run by Barry Egan (Adam Sandler) manufacture in 2002's *Punch-Drunk Love*?

■ A pudding     ■ B mattresses     ■ C harmoniums     ■ D toilet plungers

**39** This *Saving Private Ryan* player portrayed both race car driver Dale Earnhardt and baseball player Roger Maris in two different TV movies.
A. Barry Pepper
B. Ed Burns
C. Jeremy Davies
D. Matt Damon

**40** What high school football team does Billy Bob Thornton coach in 2004's *Friday Night Lights*?

**41** Where did the band the Killers get its name from?

A. a Joy Division video
B. a Duran Duran video
C. a New Order video
D. a Cure video

**42** Where does *Scrubs* star Zach Braff's directorial debut, *Garden State*, take place?

**43** On *The O.C.*, what was the name of the holiday invented by Seth Cohen?
A. ChristmasLights
B. Chrismukkah
C. ChrisKringlekah
D. Festivus

**44** David Krumholtz, star of TV's *Numb3rs*, played a stoner in which 2004 cult hit?

**45** Where did the real "Miracle on Ice"—the basis for the 2004 Kurt Russell flick *Miracle*—take place?

**46** Who dazzled the fashion world in 2001 when she wore a swan dress to the Academy Awards?

# 47

My stunts have included being encased in a New York City sidewalk, encased in a six-ton block of ice, and suspended above the Thames in a Plexiglas box. Who am I?

Answer:

# 48 What is the alias of the European master thief in 2004's Ocean's Twelve?

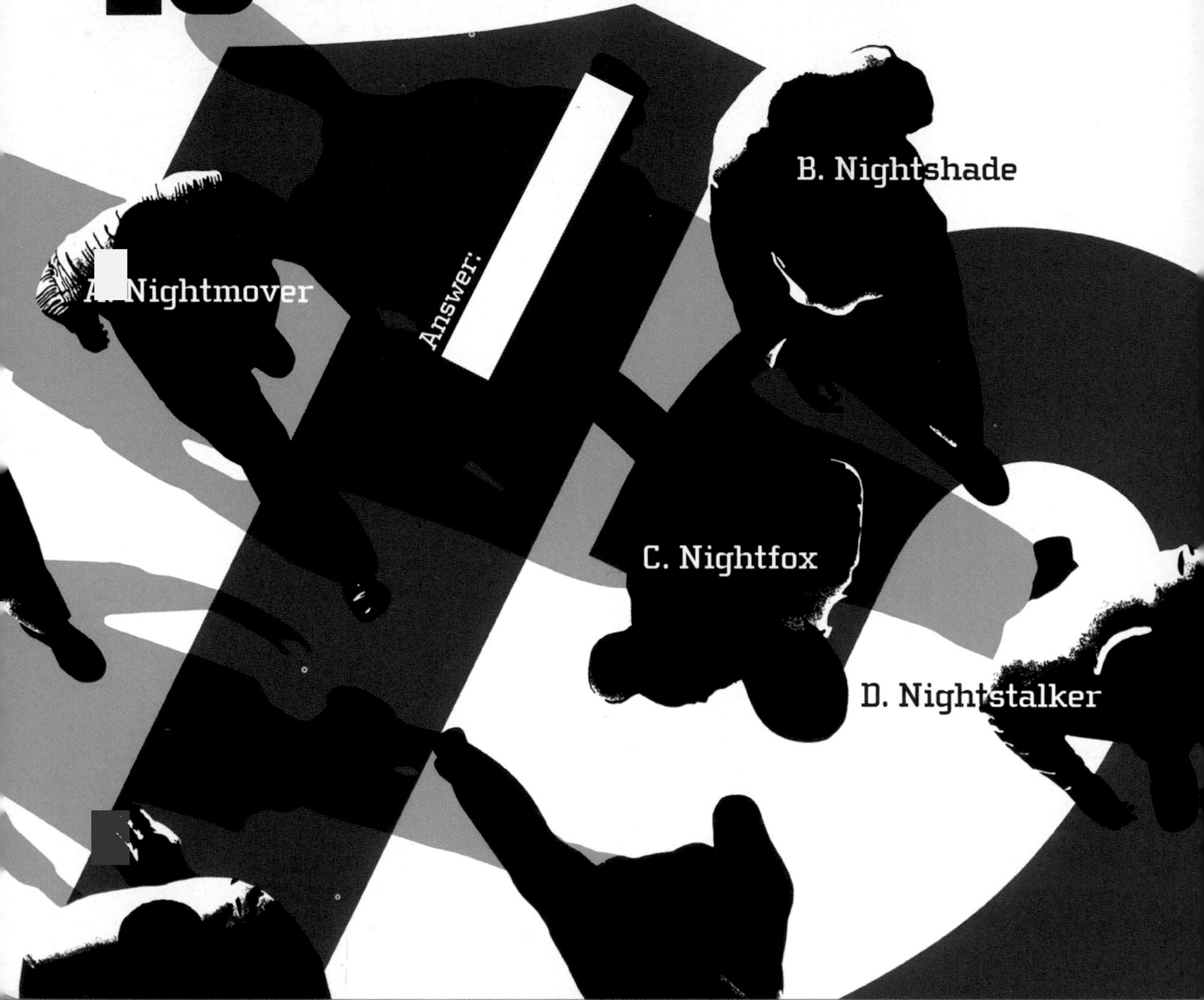

Answer:

A. Nightmover

B. Nightshade

C. Nightfox

D. Nightstalker

**49** Who sang the hit song from *O Brother, Where Art Thou?*, "I Am a Man of Constant Sorrow"?

A. Adam Steffey
B. Ricky Skaggs
C. Dan Tyminski
D. Ralph Stanley

**50** In *Everwood*, which prestigious music institution does pianist Ephram (Gregory Smith) want to attend?

**51** In *Alias*, what is the name of the prophet everyone's trying to track down artifacts from?

A. Milo Rambaldi
B. Milo Rinaldi
C. Milo Vladek
D. Arvin Sloane

**52** What term was used to explain Janet Jackson's halftime breast-flashing debacle at the 2004 Super Bowl?

A fashion malfunction
B wardrobe mistake
C fashion fluke
D wardrobe malfunction

# Ultimate Fan Challenge:

You know who you are. You sat through the trilogy—twice. You coughed up more than $100 for the special extended DVD edition. Now let's see what you really know about *The Lord of the Rings*.

**1** Who was originally cast in the role of Aragorn (the role played by Viggo Mortensen) but left shortly after shooting began?
A. Daniel Day-Lewis
B. Stuart Townsend
C. Keanu Reeves
D. Johnny Depp

**2** Besides Frodo (Elijah Wood), who were the other Hobbits along for the trip?

**3** Where is the Fellowship of the Ring journeying?

**4** How many Oscars did the final installment, 2003's *The Return of the King*, take home?

**5** Who is the evil lord who made the all-powerful One Ring?

**6** Which cast member was deemed "ineligible" for an Oscar nomination? Why?

**7** Who is Aragorn's Elvish love?

**8** What did Gollum (Andy Serkis) call the ring he so desperately wanted back?

**9** In *The Fellowship of the Ring*, what gift does Galadriel (Cate Blanchett) give to Frodo?
A. the light of Lothlorien
B. the light of Earendil
C. the light of Rivendell
D. the light of Moria

**10** The Elvish inscription on the title ring declares
A. A ring to bind them all
B. One ring to rule them all
C. This ring will rule supreme
D. A ring to win it all

# The Lord of the Rings

## 53
**In Clint Eastwood's Million Dollar Baby, what does *mo cuishle* mean?**

Answer:

**54** What 2005 Broadway musical was also a 1994 film starring Winona Ryder?

**55** What Broadway blockbuster features the song "Springtime for Hitler"?

**56** Who was the first *Survivor* contestant to land a starring film role?

**57** In 2001, it was discovered that the film critic who was quoted in ads praising Sony movies such as *Hollow Man*, *Vertical Limit*, and *The Animal* was actually the concoction of a marketing exec. What was the phony name that was used?
A. Josh Bernstein
B. David Manning
C. Thomas Lee
D. Jason Clark

**58** The making of what classic movie was the basis for 2000's *Shadow of the Vampire*, starring Willem Dafoe and John Malkovich?
A. *Nosferatu*
B. *Dracula*
C. *Frankenstein*
D. *Vampyr*

# 59

The title Eternal Sunshine of the Spotless Mind was taken from which famous poet?

A. John Keats

B. William Wordsworth

C. Lord Byron

D. Alexander Pope

Answer:

# 60

True or False?
In 2000,
singer
Melissa
Etheridge and
partner
Julie Cypher
revealed that
Graham Nash
is the father
of their son,
Beckett, and
daughter,
Bailey.

?

?

Answer:

**61** What is the musical instrument that Captain Jack Aubrey (Russell Crowe) plays in 2003's *Master and Commander: The Far Side of the World*?

A. piano
B. violin
C. cello
D. bongos

**62** New York Giants defensive back Jason Sehorn proposed to actress girlfriend Angie Harmon (*Law & Order*) on which TV show?

A. *The Late Show*
B. *The Tonight Show*
C. *Larry King Live*
D. *The Oprah Winfrey Show*

**63** Which actor interviewed President Clinton in April 2000 for an ABC Earth Day special?

A. Ben Affleck
B. Leonardo DiCaprio
C. Warren Beatty
D. Matt Damon

**64** What is the name of Drew Barrymore's dog—the one that saved her life when her Beverly Hills home was ravaged by fire?

■ A Flossie    ■ B Templeton    ■ C Fleur    ■ D Tori

**65** During a free concert she gave in 2000, Madonna flaunted a T-shirt touting which rival pop star?

**66** On The WB's *Dawson's Creek*, how did Dawson's (James Van Der Beek) father, Mitch (John Wesley Shipp), die?

**67** LL Cool J starred in 2002's *Rollerball* as well as 2003's *S.W.A.T.* What is his name (sort of) an acronym for?

A. Ladies Love Cool Joe
B. Ladies Love Cool John
C. Ladies Love Cool Jones
D. Ladies Love Cool James

# 68

Who are the only two actors to appear in all six of the **Star Wars** films, including 2005's **Star Wars: Episode III— Revenge of the Sith**?

A. Requiem for a Dream

B. Almost Famous

**69** "Purple in the morning, blue in the afternoon, orange in the evening." This is a line of dialogue from which movie?

C. Vanilla Sky

D. Minority Report

**70** What does CSI stand for?

Answer:

**71** Which *Survivor* contestant posed nude for *Playboy* in 2001?

**72** Which 'N Sync member was in talks in 2002 with Rosaviakosmos, the Russian aviation and space agency, to hitch a ride on a commercial flight to an international space station? Was it Lance, JC, or Justin?

**73** On *Desperate Housewives*, what does Bree (Marcia Cross) inadvertently put in her husband's salad that almost kills him?
A. onions
B. peppers
C. peanuts
D. shellfish

**74** What company did Tom Hanks's Chuck Noland work for before he became a *Cast Away*?

# 75

While stranded on a desert island in that same film, what improvised tool does Noland employ to extract his decayed tooth?

**A.**
tire iron

**B.**
ice skate blade

**C.**
violin bow

**D.**
golf club

# 76

Lindsay
Lohan
and
Hilary
Duff
feuded
over
what
teen
heart-
throb?

■ A. Wilmer Valderrama   ■ B. Nick Carter   ■ C. Aaron Carter   ■ D. Chris Kirkpatrick

**77** In a 2000 film, I was "father to a murdered son, husband to a murdered wife, and I will have my vengeance." Who am I?

**78** On *Six Feet Under*, what does Brenda's (Rachel Griffiths) tattoo say?

**79** What famous motivational speaker hypnotizes Hal (Jack Black) in an elevator, allowing him to see a woman's inner beauty in 2001's *Shallow Hal*?

**80** What is the all-purpose cure in 2002's *My Big Fat Greek Wedding*?

**81** Also from *My Big Fat Greek Wedding*, what boy-band member plays Toula's (Nia Vardalos) cousin?

**82** After viewing the videotape, how long before you—gulp—die in The Ring?

Answer:

**83** What was the real name of the first Joe Millionaire?

Answer:

# Answers

# So do you really know as much about pop culture as you thought you did? Check your answers against ours and find out!

## 1960s

1. B. cousin
2. "Daisy Bell (A Bicycle Built for Two)"
3. "One Last Kiss"
4. A. Florence Ballard
5. KAOS
6. believe
7. *Guess Who's Coming to Dinner*
8. Martin Luther King Jr.
9. flying rubber
10. $40,000
11. A 3, B 4, C 1, D 2
12. Dick York and Dick Sargent
13. D. 5 years
14. James Thurber
15. *for a three-hour tour, a three-hour tour.*
16. "Where have you gone?"
17. Sleepy Jean
18. B. "Good Lovin'"
19. B. Major T. J. "King" Kong
20. *The Andy Griffith Show*
21. A. 5¢
22. Marni Nixon
23. "The rain in Spain stays mainly in the plain."
24. *Who's Afraid of Virginia Woolf?*
25. Mark Lindsay
26. Buddy Sorrell and Sally Rogers
27. C. New Rochelle, New York
28. False. Later in the series, he sometimes noticed the ottoman and skipped past it.
29. Millie and Jerry Helper
30. the ceee-ment pond
31. Krakatoa is actually west of Java.
32. Nico
33. E. Desi Arnaz
34. San Francisco
35. Mr. Giles French
36. twins Buffy and Jody Davis
37. the Hollies
38. C. Rawhide
39. Oddjob
40. A 2, B 1, C 4, D 3
41. A. Elroy
42. C. a boy
43. Bodega Bay
44. *Bonnie and Clyde*
45. Fellini's *La Dolce Vita*
46. *Gidget*
47. C. P. L. Travers
48. Frostbite Falls, Minnesota
49. Rocket J. Squirrel
50. *Stranger in a Strange Land*
51. B. the Baxters
52. tape will self-destruct in five seconds
53. *The Hustler*
54. *The Flintstones*
55. Billie Joe MacAllister
56. C. the Penguin
57. drugs, specifically pills
58. A 2, B 3, C 1, D 4
59. B. remove a blood clot
60. in the knothole of a tree
61. Herman's Hermits
62. Peter Noone
63. They were both voiced by Mel Blanc.
64. Cocoa Beach, Florida

**ULTIMATE FAN CHALLENGE**

1. D. "All My Loving"
2. Pete Best
3. true
4. Liverpool
5. *A Hard Day's Night, Help!, Let It Be,* and *Yellow Submarine*
6. John Lennon, in 1967's *How I Won the War*
7. scrambled eggs
8. Jesus Christ
9. A. Stuart Sutcliffe
10. 1969's *Abbey Road*
65. C. the Amboy Dukes
66. A. *Hullabaloo*
67. *The Courtship of Eddie's Father*
68. D. Jacques
69. A. Harry Nilsson
70. Parker and Barrow
71. *Butch Cassidy and the Sundance Kid*

72. E. all of the above
73. "Build Me Up Buttercup"
74. "You rang?"
75. *Car 54, Where Are You?*
76. A. (1963), C. (1964), B. (1965)
77. Annette Funicello and Frankie Avalon
78. False. Hadji was Jonny's best friend. Their dog was called Bandit.
79. Mr. Gladstone
80. C. Snuffleupagus
81. A 2, B 3, C 4, D 1
82. B. Carl Smith
83. D. Gregory Peck (for *To Kill a Mockingbird*)
84. B. Esperanto
85. Cat
86. B. Ponchielli's *Dance of the Hours*
87. B. Stephen Stills
88. New York's Plaza hotel
89. Ken Berry
90. D. Bethel
91. D. Charley
92. A. Idaho
93. C. *Cool Hand Luke*
94. B. "I Can See for Miles"
95. Ernestine
96. Mr. Veedal, who later turned out to be author Gore Vidal
97. And that's the truth.
98. Richard Nixon
99. Edith Ann
100. yes, in the 1967 series finale with 30 million viewers watching
101. B. Tim Matheson
102. Hooterville

103. *Cleopatra*
104. *Viva Las Vegas*
105. C. Mitzi Gaynor
106. a killer doll on a 1963 episode of *The Twilight Zone*
107. Tom & Jerry
108. George Lazenby
109. B. the Rolling Stones
110. D. the Dave Clark Five, fifteen times
111. A 4, B 3, C 1, D 2
112. millionaire Bruce Wayne and his ward Dick Grayson
113. A. red
114. *McHale's Navy*
115. *Heidi*
116. D. Florida
117. D. a would-be assassin's bullet
118. C. Frank Sinatra
119. C. the Dillards
120. C. seven

## 1970s

1. Maureen McGovern
2. the World Series
3. B. Norman Fell
4. Priscilla Barnes
5. B. Eagles
6. A. Jeff Goldblum
7. True. Production began with Young in the role.
8. Mary
9. D. the Question
10. A 2, B 3, C 1, D 4
11. C. 138 stories
12. "Midnight Train to Georgia"

13. Dr. Steven Kiley
14. Barry Manilow
15. *Dog Day Afternoon*
16. False (but he's hosted thirteen times and made many guest appearances)
17. Chuckles the Clown's funeral
18. "Because the Night"
19. He was a photographer.
20. the Cowsills
21. A. Harvard and Radcliffe
22. "Mockingbird"
23. Madeline Kahn, playing Dr. Frankenstein's fiancée Elizabeth
24. Gene Hackman
25. B. senator
26. B. Tiny Tim
27. B. Tiger crashed through it.
28. the Ditmeyers
29. A. Kitty KarryAll
30. C. Oliver
31. Alice
32. Sam
33. Jean Stapleton (for her role as Edith Bunker) in 1971
34. He was his son-in-law.
35. Deltas and Omegas
36. C. Fred
37. *Bananas* and *Sleeper*
38. producer-director Irwin Allen
39. World Trade Center
40. B. pro football quarterback
41. Schneider
42. A 4, B 3, C 1, D 2
43. A 2, B 4, C 1, D 3
44. Hot Lips and Ferret Face

45. Radar O'Reilly
46. A. *The Bells of St. Mary's*
47. Arthur
48. C. Killer
49. Amity Island
50. Pat Morita
51. C. *Rhoda*
52. one
53. *Rich Man, Poor Man*
54. Cat Stevens
55. B. Jack Albertson
56. Katharine Ross
57. B. Richard Nixon
58. D. Mia Farrow
59. A. *A Clockwork Orange*
60. coca leaves
61. the Sunshine Cab Company
62. Carole King's *Tapestry*
63. Nixon
64. *Fernwood 2-Night*
65. Janis Joplin
66. B. Max

**ULTIMATE FAN CHALLENGE**

1. C. Rags
2. *Manhattan*
3. Marshall McLuhan
4. B. San Marcos
5. snow
6. *Play It Again, Sam*
7. another woman
8. Meryl Streep
9. 1978's *Interiors*
10. D. "Most of us need the eggs."
11. D. Two
67. five; Charlie, Veruca Salt, Mike Teevee, Augustus Gloop, and Violet Beauregarde
68. C. *Jesus of Cool*
69. *Happy Days* (from an episode in which Fonzie actually water-skis over a shark)
70. C. Gram Parsons
71. B. Bernard Shakey
72. Jimmie "J.J." Walker
73. Charlie Chaplin
74. D. divorce
75. Uncle Owen and Aunt Beru
76. He's hiding after accidentally killing a girl.
77. B. horse racing
78. the Eagles' in 1975; the Emotions' was in '77.
79. Mother
80. A. pea soup
81. *The Daily Planet*
82. Kal-El
83. B. Bernice
84. A. Talking Heads
85. B. Paddy Chayefsky
86. "Nanu, nanu"
87. Jack Lord as Detective Steve McGarrett
88. *Dance Fever*
89. *The Towering Inferno*
90. It was shown in seat-shaking Sensurround.
91. B. 1972
92. D. Penny Marshall
93. D. George Carlin
94. San Francisco
95. Gene Siskel
96. "A long time ago in a galaxy far, far away..."
97. contact (for the record, a close encounter of the first kind is a UFO sighting; a close encounter of the second kind is physical evidence of an alien landing)
98. 1. Brian Jones, 2. Keith Richards, 3. Mick Taylor, and 4. Ron Wood
99. A. 1970
100. Howard Cosell, Keith Jackson, and Don Meredith
101. Pink Floyd's *Dark Side of the Moon*
102. C. Ted
103. Barbara Walters
104. C. *Babel*
105. C. junkyard
106. He asks for an omelet, plain.
107. *Maude*
108. Chuck Barris
109. *McCloud*
110. A. *Checking In*
111. *Kojak*

## 1980s

1. South Bend Central
2. D. "The Breathing Method"
3. Elliot Ness
4. Coy and Vance
5. Robin Masters
6. Orson Welles
7. *Carpe diem!*
8. B. Welton Academy
9. Hillman College
10. *The Cosby Show*
11. "Danke Schoen" and

# Answers

"Twist and Shout"

12. C. Fenway Park

13. A. get a Slushie

14 A. Susanna Hoffs of the Bangles

15. Jimmy Smits was Eddie Rivera.

16. C. Mypos

17. B. brothers

18. D. Alfred Uhry (for *Driving Miss Daisy*)

19. *Empty Nest*

20. A. diamond earrings

21. A. a bunny

22. Penny Marshall with 1988's *Big*

23. Stephen Bishop

24. Erika Eleniak

25. B. Zoltar

26. A 3, B 4, C 1, D 2

27. Gus Grissom

28. on the side

29. C. Ann-Margret

30. the New York Yankees

31. Bushwood

32. alien life form

33. Gordon Shumway

34. B. Melmac

35. B. "Ha, I kill me."

36. True. His cohost was Ed McMahon, and he had such guests as Eric Roberts and Vincent Pastore.

37. Lucky

38. A. cancer

39. Senator Lloyd Bentsen

40. He played John Belushi in *Wired*.

41. *Broadcast News*

42. B. Peter Gallagher

43. in a bizarre gardening accident

44. He choked on someone else's vomit.

45. D. Barbara Billingsley (aka Beaver Cleaver's mom)

46. B. *Southwest General*

47. Ted Danson (although Tom Selleck would marry little Mary's mom in the sequel, *Three Men and a Little Lady*)

48. *Angel Heart*

49. Neil Diamond

50. *Cheers*

51. *Fridays*

52. her diamond earring

53. Skippy Handleman (played by Marc Price)

54. 1988's *Just the Ten of Us*

55. B. Marilyn Monroe

56. 1985's *St. Elmo's Fire*

57. *Too Close for Comfort*

58. C. Carnegie Deli

59. D. unknown

60. *Rocky III*

61. at the Philadelphia Museum of Art

62. Calvin Klein

63. A. Jimi Hendrix

64. B. 1.21 gigawatts

65. B. Mel Tormé

66. Stephanie Zimbalist

67. C. human being

68. B. "Dust in the Wind"

## ULTIMATE FAN CHALLENGE

1. a snipe

2. Melville's

3. *Jeopardy!*

4. a couple of chins

5. "O Canada"

6. He's run over by a Zamboni machine.

7. Milk-Bone underwear

8. a bottle cap (from the last beer he ever drank)

9. C. plumber

10. D. Kirstie Alley

11. A 2, B 1, C 4, D 3

69. True. Indy always kept his hat on for production continuity. It actually becomes a running joke throughout the film.

70. John Lithgow

71. A. Robin Williams

72. Susan Sontag

73. George Harrison, Roy Orbison, Jeff Lynne, Tom Petty, and Bob Dylan

74. *Cocktail*

75. in the Florida Keys

76. A. *Gandhi*

77. A. "Heartbeat"

78. arm wrestling

79. Phil Collins

80. Michael J. Fox

81. C. Rosie O'Donnell

82. A 4, B 3, C 2, D 1

83. John Cusack

84. Karen Carpenter

85. D. Bill Murray

86. D. touching her two index fingers together

87. Vincent Price

88. "as you wish"

89. A. *Ghostbusters II*
90. St. Olaf
91. B. Dana Barrett (Sigourney Weaver)
92. Daniel Day-Lewis
93. A. *Silkwood*
94. *The Tracey Ullman Show*
95. A. a strip club
96. Roy Rogers
97. A 3, B 2, C 1
98 D. Humphrey Bogart
99. Bud
100. the American flag
101. C. Meryl Streep
102. Jeremy Piven
103. "Heartlight"
104. C. Adrian Cronauer
105. A 3, B 2, C 4, D 1
106. It multiplies.
107. true
108. Meg Ryan
109. *Full House*
110. *The Fly*
111. C. $1
112. A. *Ordinary People*
113. Lionel Richie
114. Camp Crystal Lake
115. *American Gigolo*
116. D. banana
117. I'm just drawn that way
118. Jessica Rabbit
119. D. Tina Turner
120. A. He-Man (*Masters of the Universe*)
121. Tom Servo and Crow T. Robot
122. C. flying

123. "Love Buzz"
124. C. Berkeley Breathed
125. That's "the year we make contact."
126. Joan Rivers
127. *Stripes, Ghostbusters,* and *Ghostbusters II*
128. D. Sylvester Stallone
129. *St. Elsewhere*
130. C. Fred Grandy
131. Whitley Strieber
132. C. Stephen King
133. A 3, B 1, C 4, D 2
134. Bud and Kelly

## 1990s

1. Daniel Stern
2. Jessica Savitch
3. C. Santa Maria
4. A. *Barton Fink*
5. She stabs him with her stiletto heel.
6. *What's Eating Gilbert Grape*
7. Robert Urich
8. *Weir'd Tales*
9. Penny Marshall
10. B. Turkish
11. Wilson
12. A 3, B 2, C 1
13. D. Dorothy
14. the lavender bus
15. *Saturday Night Live*
16. B. Princess Diana
17. Patsy Cline
18. 1999's *Fight Club*
19. B. measles

20. Digitally darkening Simpson's skin tone. The magazine later explained that the picture was a "photo illustration."
21. In the novel, she chops off one of his feet with an ax.
22. D. Elvis Presley
23. *Ellen*
24. Veronica Lake
25. C. Amanda (played by Heather Locklear)
26. to Hugh Grant, when he appeared on the show after the Divine Brown scandal
27. C. *The Third Man*
28. River Phoenix
29. C. Aretha Franklin
30. A. Mr. Smiley's
31. John Goodman
32. *F.Y.I.*
33. comedian Andy Kaufman
34. coffee-flavored beer
35. True. It was made for The Simpsons House Giveaway contest and won by Barbara Howard, a sixty-three-year-old grandmother, in 1997.
36. D. Pennsylvania
37. B. "Hard Luck Woman"
38. A. Initech
39. Elvis Presley
40. B. Randall Stephens
41. C. a drinking/grenade game
42. Nicole Eggert
43. Alyssa Milano
44. *Titanic*

45. B. Tim Robbins
46. death's-head moth
47. A 1, B 2, C 3, D 4
48. Dolores
49. Seven (Mickey Mantle's number)
50. Kramer, Elaine, Jerry, George
51. licking toxic glue on cheap wedding invitation envelopes
52. B. Isosceles
53. A 3, B 1, C 2, D 4
54. Jerry (because George admitted that he lied)
55. Lester Bangs
56. Haley Joel Osment
57. B. Phil Collins
58. A. three
59. the interview! He's fleeing the interview!
60. B. "Baby Did a Bad Bad Thing"
61. C. USS *Alabama*
62. Patrick Swayze
63. *Beverly Hills, 90210*
64. Arthur Kent
65. B. La Brea Tar Pits
66. director James Cameron
67. to be really handsome, as in any one of the acting Baldwin brothers
68. A. Cincinnati Reds
69. *Ned and Stacey*
70. C. computer virus
71. cut off its head
72. Mr. Jingles
73. *The Indian Runner*
74. A. Alice Cooper
75. A 3, B 4, C 5, D 2, E 1
76. David Cross and Bob Odenkirk

77. C. Steven Spielberg
78. 10,000 Maniacs
79. D. Cate Blanchett
80. 1995's *Goldeneye*
81. Manchester
82. *In Living Color*
83. D. Café Nervosa
84. *The Two Jakes*
85. Tammy Wynette
86. *Courage Under Fire*

ULTIMATE FAN CHALLENGE
1. VD
2. B. "The Lion Sleeps Tonight"
3. Isabella Rossellini (but he'd already taken her off his list)
4. C. Minsk
5. "Copacabana"
6. in the Museum of Natural History
7. Yemen
8. Dr. Drake Ramoray
9. Mockolate
10. the Rembrandts
87. B. 12
88. B. August 29, 1997
89. A. violin
90. "You Gotta Be"
91. C. Pennsylvania
92. A. KEG
93. *True Love*
94. B. *Toy Story*
95. *Evita*
96. Rick Schroder
97. C. Jean-Pierre Jeunet
98. *Arlington Road*
99. *Titanic*

100. Cindy Crawford
101. Art Shamsky
102. lemon chicken
103. A. Winona Ryder
104. velociraptor
105. a food critic
106. D. George Foreman Grill
107. B. Kathy Bates
108. C. eighteen
109. D. Monet
110. C. Soul Asylum
111. B. Erie, Pennsylvania
112. The Oneders
113. 1993's *Rising Sun*
114. D. Martin Scorsese
115. being a cobbler
116. C. Aimee Mann
117. B. *Wag the Dog*
118. D. Jay
119. C. Natalie Imbruglia, who was born in Sydney, Australia
120. Mr. Pointy
121. Garbage
122. Wilson Pickett
123. one-armed push-ups
124. D. Scottie Pippen
125. Smoothaise
126. A. Dean & DeLuca

## 2000s

1. Esther
2. B. Julia Roberts
3. *The Lone Gunmen*
4. Bill Murray
5. "You stay classy, San Diego."
6. C. Silencio

7. the Everly Brothers

8. Ted Nugent

9. A. Fred Armisen

10. A. Waldorf, Maryland

11. "Bartlet for America"

12. C. New Hampshire

13. Michael Caine

14. B. Bonesaw

15. He won the lottery with them.

16. C. Ja Rule

17. B. They were all born in Delaware.

18. B. Ravi Shankar

19. Sir Laurence Olivier

20. merlot

21. C. 74

22. What is H&R Block?

23. D. Chris Matthews

24. *Once and Again*

25. fashion roadkill

26. a Post-it

27. She fell in front of a taxi in which he was riding.

28. B. Alanis Morissette

29. John

30. Miranda

31. C. Horace Green

32. 2001's *A.I. Artificial Intelligence,* 2002's *Minority Report,* and 2002's *Catch Me If You Can*

33. Cate Blanchett

34. Phinnaeus and Hazel

35. Sploosh!

36. A. Silvio

37. Tokyo

38. D. toilet plungers

39. A. Barry Pepper, who was in 3: *The Dale Earnhardt Story* and *61**

40. Permian High School Panthers of Odessa, Texas

41. C. a New Order video

42. New Jersey

43. B. Chrismukkah

44. *Harold & Kumar Go to White Castle*

45. at the 1980 Winter Olympics in Lake Placid

46. Björk

47. David Blaine

48. C. Nightfox

49. C. Dan Tyminski

50. Juilliard

51. A. Milo Rambaldi

52. D. wardrobe malfunction

**ULTIMATE FAN CHALLENGE**

1. B. Stuart Townsend

2. Samwise, Merry, and Pippin

3. to Mordor/Mount Doom to destroy the ring

4. eleven

5. Sauron

6. Andy Serkis, who portrayed Gollum, because his character on-screen was computer generated

7. Arwen (Liv Tyler)

8. the Precious

9. B. the light of Earendil

10. B. One ring to rule them all

53. "my darling" or "my Love"

54. *Little Women*

55. *The Producers*

56. Colleen Haskell, from *Survivor: Borneo*, played the love interest in the Rob Schneider 2001 comedy *The Animal.*

57. B. David Manning

58. A. *Nosferatu*

59. D. Alexander Pope

60. False. They revealed that the father is Nash's longtime duo partner, David Crosby.

61. B. violin

62. B. *The Tonight Show*

63. B. Leonardo DiCaprio

64. A. Flossie

65. Britney Spears

66. car accident

67. D. Ladies Love Cool James

68. Anthony Daniels (C-3PO) and Kenny Baker (R2-D2)

69. A. *Requiem for a Dream*

70. Crime Scene Investigation

71. Jerri Manthey, from *Survivor: The Australian Outback*

72. Lance Bass

73. A. onions

74. Federal Express

75. B. ice skate blade

76. C. Aaron Carter

77. *Gladiator's* Maximus

78. Nathaniel

79. Tony Robbins

80. Windex

81. Joey Fatone of 'N Sync

82. seven days

83. Evan Marriott

**1960s** p. 6: Everett Collection (The Andy Griffith Show); Columbia/The Kobal Collection (Bye Bye Birdie); Cyrus Andrews/Redferns/Retna Ltd. (The Supremes); Everett Collection (Get Smart; Tracy); p. 7: Everett Collection; p. 8: Everett Collection (4); p. 9: Everett Collection (The Lucy Show); Everett Collection (Denver); David Redfern/Redferns/Retna Ltd. (Simon & Garfunkel); p. 10: Henry Diltz/Retna (The Monkees); Bettmann/Corbis (The Young Rascals); Everett Collection (Nabors; A Charlie Brown Christmas; Cleopatra); p. 11: Authenticated News/Getty Images; p. 12: Everett Collection; p. 13: Everett Collection (Amsterdam and Rose Marie); CBS/Photofest (Van Dyke and Moore); Gabi Rona/MPTV.net (Guilbert and Paris); p. 14: Everett Collection (Beverly Hillbillies; Krakatoa, East of Java; Family Affair; Goldfinger); Henry Diltz/Corbis (McKenzie; Nash); p. 15: Everett Collection (Who's Afraid of Virginia Woolf?; Funny Girl); 20th Century Fox/Courtesy Everett Collection (Planet of the Apes); Columbia Pictures/Photofest (Dr. Strangelove); p. 16: ABC/Photofest; p. 17: Universal/The Kobal Collection (The Birds); Everett Collection (Field; Mary Poppins); p. 18: Everett Collection (5); p. 19: MichaelOchsArchives.com (The Chantels); Robert Vincett/Redferns/Retna Ltd. (The Ronettes); Frank Driggs Collection/Getty Images (The Chiffons); Ron Case/Getty Images (The Shangri-Las); p. 20: 20th Century Fox/The Kobal Collection; p. 21: Everett Collection (3); p. 22: Apple Corps Ltd./Everett Collection (Liverpool); Underwood & Underwood/Corbis (Beatles); Bettmann/Corbis (album burning; Sutcliffe); p. 23: Everett Collection; p. 24: MichaelOchsArchives.com (Amboy Dukes); Chris Walter/Wireimage.com (Nugent); p. 25: Everett Collection (Hullabaloo; Sellers); Henry Diltz/Corbis (Three Dog Night); RB/Redferns/Retna Ltd. (King); Harry Goodwin/MichaelOchsArchives.com (The Foundations); p. 26: MPTV.net (The Addams Family); Everett Collection (Lewis); Embassy Pictures/Courtesy Everett Collection (Rae); Embassy/The Kobal Collection (The Graduate); p. 27: Sesame Workshop (5); p. 28: NBC/Gene Trindl/Photofest (Kelley); Paramount/Courtesy Everett Collection (Doohan); Paramount/ Television/The Kobal Collection (Takei); Everett Collection (Nichols); p. 29: Embassy/The Kobal Collection (The Graduate); Everett Collection (Lawrence of Arabia); Everett Collection (Shatner; Breakfast at Tiffany's); Paramount/The Kobal Collection (Barefoot in the Park); p. 30: Lambert/Getty Images (Woodstock); Hulton-Deutsch Collection/Corbis (Hemingway); Everett Collection (Newman); p. 31: Paul Ryan/MichaelOchsArchives.com; p. 32: The Kobal Collection; p. 33: Gabi Rona (Tomlin with phone); Lorimar/NBC-TV/The Kobal Collection (Rowan and Hawn); Everett Collection (Tomlin with rocking chair); p. 34: Everett Collection (5); p. 35: Bettmann/Corbis (Beatles with Sullivan); Everett Collection (3); p. 36: Everett Collection (4); p. 37: Everett Collection; p. 38: Everett Collection (5); p. 39: 20th Century Fox/The Kobal Collection; **1970s** p. 42: Everett Collection (The Poseidon Adventure; Three's Company; Nashville); Lynn Goldsmith/Corbis (Newman); TTI/Retna Ltd. (Springsteen); p. 43: Universal/Celandine/Monty Python/The Kobal Collection (Idle); Everett Collection (Cleese); The Kobal Collection (Palin); Eric Robert/Corbis Sygma (Jones); p. 44: The Kobal Collection; p. 45: Bettmann/Corbis (Gladys Knight and the Pips); Everett Collection (Brolin; Dog Day Afternoon); Andy Freeberg/Retna Ltd. (Steve Martin); p. 46: Everett Collection (The Mary Tyler Moore Show; Love Story); Lynn Goldsmith/Corbis (Smith); TTI/Retna Ltd. (Simon and Taylor); Universal Pictures/Photofest (Belushi); p. 47: Gai Terrell/Redferns/Retna Ltd. (John); Frank Wills/Camera Press/ Retna Ltd. (Tiny Tim); Peter Mazel/Sunshine/Retna (Mercury); Richard E. Aaron/Retna (Friedman); p. 48: Everett Collection; p. 49: The Kobal Collection (Marcia and Bobby); 49: Everett Collection (3) p. 50: MPTV.net (All in the Family); Everett Collection (Blake; Harrington Jr.); Bettmann/Corbis (Cosell); Paramount/Everett Collection (King Kong); p. 51: Baron Wolman/Retna Ltd.; p. 52: Everett Collection (4); p. 53: The Kobal Collection (3); p. 54: The Kobal Collection (Jaws); Columbia Pictures/Everett Collection (Charlie's Angels); Everett Collection (Rich Man, Poor Man; Prinze); p. 55: The Kobal Collection (A Clockwork Orange); Everett Collection (3); p. 56: Everett Collection; p. 57: Everett Collection (Fernwood Tonight); The Kobal Collection (Midler); Bettmann/Corbis (The Bionic Woman); p. 58: The Kobal Collection; p. 59: The Kobal Collection (Play It Again, Sam [2]; Annie Hall [2]; Sleeper); Bettmann/Corbis (Annie Hall); Everett Collection (Bananas; Manhattan; Love and Death) p. 60: Everett Collection; p. 61: Ian Dickson/Redferns/Retna Ltd. (Lowe); Redferns/Retna (Harris); Dick Barnatt/Redferns/Retna Ltd. (Young) p. 62: Everett Collection (Good Times; Hoffman; Lucasfilm (Star Wars); Everett Collection (The Sting); Channel 5 Broadcasting/The Kobal Collection (Alien); p. 64: 20th Century Fox/Everett Collection p. 65: Everett Collection (Barney Miller); Frank Edwards/Fotos International/Getty Images (Redgrave); Paramount/Courtesy Everett Collection (Mork & Mindy); p. 66: Everett Collection (Hawaii Five-O; American Graffiti; Dance Fever); Henry Diltz/Corbis (Jackson Browne); Paramount Pictures/The Kobal Collection (Travolta); p. 67: Paul Beard/Getty (space background); p. 68: Everett Collection ; p. 69: Peter Shillingford/Camera Press/Retna (Jones); Henry Diltz/Corbis (Richards); Michael Putland/Retna (Taylor); Denis O'Regan/Corbis (Wood); p. 70: James L. Amos/Corbis; p. 71: The Kobal Collection (Five Easy Pieces); Everett Collection (4); **1980s** p. 74: Everett Collection (Hoosiers; The Dukes of Hazzard); Paramount/Courtesy Everett Collection (The Untouchables); Touchstone/The Kobal Collection (Dead Poets Society); p. 75: Everett Collection; p. 76: Everett Collection; p. 77: New World Releasing/Courtesy Everett Collection (Heathers); Everett Collection (Johnson; Perfect Strangers); p. 78: Andora Pictures International/Everett Collection (Simon & Simon); Buena Vista Pictures/Courtesy Everett Collection (Leisure); Paramount/Courtesy Everett Collection (Some Kind of Wonderful); Warner Bros./Everett Collection (Innerspace); Everett Collection (E.T. the Extra-Terrestrial); p. 79: Brian Hamill/20th Century Fox/The Kobal Collection; p. 80: Warner Bros./The Kobal Collection (Quaid; Ward); Warner Bros./Everett Collection (Harris; Glenn); p. 81: Columbia Pictures/Courtesy Everett Collection (When Harry Met Sally...); Paramount/Courtesy Everett Collection (Major League); Orion Pictures/Courtesy Everett Collection (Caddyshack); p. 82: Everett Collection; p. 83: Everett Collection (ALF waving); MPTV.net (ALF with sandwich); p. 84: Mike Prior/Redferns/Retna (Marley); Ron Edmonds/AP (Quayle); United Artists/Courtesy Everett Collection (The Idolmaker; Tootsie); The Kobal Collection (This Is Spinal Tap); p. 85: Buena Vista Pictures/Courtesy Everett Collection; p. 86: TriStar Pictures/Everett Collection (Bonet); Everett Collection (Cosby); p. 87: E.J. Camp/Retna Ltd. (UB40); Universal/The Kobal Collection (Nelson); Everett Collection (Family Ties); p. 88: Everett Collection (Growing Pains; Gray; Knight; Rocky); Robert Phillips/Everett Collection (Hill Street Blues); Orion Pictures/Everett Collection (Broadway Danny Rose); p. 89: Baron Wolman /Retna (Hendrix); Gai Terrell/Redferns/Retna (Dylan; Brown); Doc Pele/Stills/Retna U.K. (Presley); p. 90: MCA/Courtesy Everett Collection; p. 91: Warner Bros./Everett Collection (Night Court); NBC/Courtesy Everett Collection (Remington Steele); Everett Collection (The Elephant Man); Orion Pictures/Courtesy Everett Collection (Bill & Ted's Excellent Adventure); p. 92: NBC/Courtesy Everett Collection (Wendt; Danson; Anderson); NBC/Photofest (Alley); p. 93: NBC/Photofest; p. 94: Paramount/Courtesy Everett Collection (Ford); Roger Ressmeyer/Corbis (McFerrin); Orion Pictures/Courtesy Everett Collection (Bull Durham); AP (Wilson); Dan Dion/Retna Ltd. (Nixon); p. 95: Everett Collection (McMahon); Mark Sullivan/Wireimage.com (DeGeneres); Steve Granitz/Wireimage.com (Winfrey); Jim Spellman/Wireimage.com (O'Donnell); Gregory Pace/Corbis (Rhea); p. 96: Columbia Pictures/Courtesy Everett Collection (O'Connell; Feldman); Columbia Pictures/The Kobal Collection (Wheaton; Phoenix); p. 97: C.J. Contino/Everett Collection (Haynes); Universal/Courtesy Everett Collection (Flannigan); MCA/Universal/Everett Collection ("Thriller"); p. 98: 20th Century Fox/Courtesy Everett Collection (The Princess Bride); Touchstone Television/Courtesy Everett Collection (White); Columbia Pictures/Courtesy Everett Collection (Ghostbusters); Cinecom Pictures/Courtesy Everett Collection (Bonham Carter); Everett Collection (Streep); 20th Century Fox/The Kobal Collection (Porky's); p. 99: 20th Century Fox/The Kobal Collection (Willis); Everett Collection (Lone Ranger); The Kobal Collection (Rogers; Autry); p. 100: 20th Century Fox/Courtesy Everett Collection (Haim); Columbia Pictures/Courtesy Everett Collection (Feldman); Paul Natkin/Wireimage.com (Hart); p. 101: Everett Collection (Knight Pulliam); The Kobal Collection (Say

Anything); Paul Natkin/Wireimage.com (Diamond); p. 102: Touchstone/Photofest; p. 103: Retna 5/Retna U.K. (Kajagoogoo); Fin Costello/Redferns/Retna (A Flock of Seagulls); Tony Mottram/Retna U.K. (The Escape Club); Michael Wilfling/Vanit/Retna (A-ha); p. 105: Warner Bros./Everett Collection (Gremlins); Paramount/The Kobal Collection (Edwards); Everett Collection (Full House; Trading Places); p. 105: Barry Schultz/Sunshine/Retna; p. 106: The Kobal Collection (Murphy); Davies & Starr/The Images Bank/Getty Images (grapes); Davies & Starr/Stone/Getty Images (kiwi); Tim Turner/FoodPix/Getty Images (peach); Burke/Triolo Productions/FoodPix/Getty Images (banana); p. 107: Buena Vista Pictures/Courtesy Everett Collection (Who Framed Roger Rabbit?); Miramax/Courtesy Everett Collection (Cox); Comedy Central/Courtesy Everett Collection (Mystery Science Theater 3000); p. 108: Universal/Courtesy Everett Collection (The A-Team); Berkeley Breathed (Opus); The Kobal Collection (Lithgow); Columbia Pictures/Courtesy Everett Collection (Murray); Columbia Pictures/Courtesy Everett Collection (Ramis); p. 109: Tri-Star/The Kobal Collection; p. 110: Paramount/Courtesy Everett Collection (Cruise); Artisan Entertainment/Courtesy Everett Collection (Dirty Dancing); Everett Collection (An Officer and a Gentleman; Flashdance); p. 111: Fox/Photofest; 1990s p. 114: Everett Collection (The Wonder Years); Paramount/Courtesy Everett Collection (The Truman Show); Columbia/The Kobal Collection (Leigh); MGM/Courtesy Everett Collection (DeVito); Gramercy Pictures/Courtesy Everett Collection (The Usual Suspects); p. 115: Theo Wargo/Wireimage.com (Weinberg); Kevin Winter/Getty Images (Eubanks); Everett Collection (Shaffer); CBS/Courtesy Everett Collection (Letterman); NBC/Courtesy Everett Collection (Leno; O'Brien); p. 116: Warner Bros./Courtesy Everett Collection; p. 117: Warner Bros./Courtesy Everett Collection (The Adventures of Priscilla Queen of the Desert); Steve Granitz/Wireimage.com (Costner); Susan Sterner/AP (Rimes); New Line Productions Inc./Courtesy Everett Collection (Pitt); p. 118: Universal/Courtesy Everett Collection (Sinise); Columbia Pictures/Courtesy Everett Collection (Misery); Ernie Paniccioli/Retna Ltd. (Public Enemy); Warner Bros./Everett Collection (Basinger); Everett Collection (Calabro); p. 119: Mary Ellen Matthews/NBC/AP (Pavarotti); Ron Galella/Wireimage.com (Houston); Moises Castillo/AP (Domingo); Rick Diamond/AP (Franklin); Emile Wamsteker/AP (Jewel); p. 120: DreamWorks/Courtesy Everett Collection; p. 121: Everett Collection (Bergen); Bill Cooke/AP (Estefan); Barbara Steinwehe/Redferns/Retna Ltd. (Brooks); p. 122: 20th Century Fox/Courtesy Everett Collection (Office Space); Gramercy Pictures/Courtesy Everett Collection (Robbins); Universal/Courtesy Everett Collection (Scent of a Woman); New Line Productions Inc./Courtesy Everett Collection (Barrymore); Orion Pictures/Courtesy Everett Collection (Foster); p. 123: Louis Goldman/Columbia/The Kobal Collection (Madonna); Columbia/The Kobal Collection (Petty); Everett Collection (Davis; O'Donnell); p. 124: Castle Rock Entertainment/Courtesy Everett Collection; p. 125: Columbia Tristar/Courtesy Everett Collection (Alexander); Everett Collection (Richards); Steve Granitz/Wireimage.com (Davis); Sam Levi/Wireimage.com (Garofalo); Michelson/Globe Photos (Leeves); Ron Galella/Wireimage.com (Hatcher); p. 126: DreamWorks/Courtesy Everett Collection (Almost Famous); Phillip Caruso/Paramount/The Kobal Collection (Forrest Gump); Gramercy Pictures/Courtesy Everett Collection (McDormand); p. 127: Warner Bros./Everett Collection (Eyes Wide Shut); Jim Cooper/Retna (Isaak); p. 128: Richard Foreman/Hollywood Pictures/The Kobal Collection; p. 129: Everett Collection (Farley); 20th Century Fox/Courtesy Everett Collection (Volcano); 20th Century Fox/Courtesy Everett Collection (Titanic); Paramount/Courtesy Everett Collection (Clueless); Jim Smeal/Wireimage.com (Messing); 20th Century Fox/Courtesy Everett Collection (Independence Day); p. 130: Everett Collection (Highlander); The Kobal Collection (The Green Mile; Myers); p. 131: Fernando Aceves/Retna Ltd. (Morissette); Bob Spencer/Retna (Jewel); Jay Blakesberg/Retna (Osborne); Kelly Swift/Retna (Cole); R. Collaris/Sunshine/Retna U.K. (Amos); p. 132: Everett Collection (Mr. Show); p. 133: Everett Collection (Gable); United Artists/Courtesy Everett Collection (Brosnan); Fox/Photofest (Carrey); NBC/Courtesy Everett Collection (Frasier); 20th Century Fox/Courtesy Everett Collection (Washington); p. 134: NBC/Courtesy Everett Collection (3); p. 135: Warner Bros./Everett Collection; p. 136: Sidney Baldwin/Regency Entertainment; p. 137: Everett Collection (Terminator 2: Judgment Day; Chabert); Paramount/Courtesy Everett Collection (Robbins); Everett Collection (Beverly Hills, 90210); p. 138: Columbia TriStar Television/Courtesy Everett Collection (Dawson's Creek); Walt Disney Co./Courtesy Everett Collection (A Bug's Life); 20th Century Fox/Courtesy Everett Collection (Alien: Resurrection); Everett Collection (Arlington Road; Garrett); p. 139: Ron Galella/Wireimage.com (Leary); Miramax/Courtesy Everett Collection (4); p. 140: Everett Collection; p. 141: TriStar Pictures/Courtesy Everett Collection (My Best Friend's Wedding); Walt Disney Co./Courtesy Everett Collection (Travolta); Ben Luzon/AP (Lucci); p. 142: Barry Wetcher/United Artists; 143: Neal Preston/Corbis; p. 144: 20th Century Fox/Courtesy Everett Collection (That Thing That You Do!; Rising Sun); Tom Mendoza/LADN/Wireimage.com (Day-Lewis); New Line Productions Inc./Courtesy Everett Collection (Magnolia); Fox/Photofest (The Simpsons); p. 145: 20th Century Fox/Courtesy Everett Collection; p. 146: Bureau L.A. Collection/Corbis (Nirvana); Myriam Santos-Kayda/Retna (Vig); p. 147: The Kobal Collection (The Commitments); Stephen Dunn/Allsport/Getty (Bird); Everett Collection (Russell); 2000s p. 150: Armando Gallo/Retna Ltd. (Madonna); DreamWorks/Courtesy Everett Collection (Anchorman); Matt Dunham/Reuters/Corbis (Simon & Garfunkel); p. 151: Jason Squires/Wireimage.com (Blue Man Group); James Devaney/Wireimage.com (Armisen); Jim Spellman/Wireimage.com (Hammond); Jeffrey Mayer/Wireimage.com (Forte); Johnny Nunez/Wireimage.com (Meyers); p. 152: Camera Press/Jenny Lewis/Retna Ltd.; p. 153: NBC/Courtesy Everett Collection (Sheen); New Line/Courtesy Everett Collection (Myers); Columbia Pictures/Courtesy Everett Collection (Spider-Man); p. 154: ABC/Courtesy Everett Collection (Lost); Scott D. Smith/Retna Ltd. (Jones); AP (Jennings); Charles Dharapak/AP (Miller); p. 155: Warner Bros./Everett Collection; p. 156: HBO/Courtesy Everett Collection; p. 157: HBO/Courtesy Everett Collection (4); p. 158: Paramount/Courtesy Everett Collection; p. 159: Lester Cohen/Wireimage.com (Spielberg); Paramount/Courtesy Everett Collection (Pacino); Yoshio Sato/Focus Features (Lost in Translation); p. 160: Columbia Pictures/Courtesy Everett Collection (Sandler); Ralph Nelson/Universal Studios (Thornton); Pamela Littky/Retna Ltd. (The Killers); Warner Bros./Courtesy Everett Collection (The O.C.); Steve Granitz/Wireimage.com (Björk); p. 161: Rune Hellestad/Corbis; p. 162: Warner Bros./Courtesy Everett Collection; p. 163: Walt Disney Co./Courtesy Everett Collection (O Brother, Where Art Thou?); Everett Collection (Everwood); Norman Jean Roy/Touchstone Television (Garner); Pierre Ducharme/Reuters/Corbis (Jackson and Timberlake); p. 164: New Line Productions Inc. (3); p. 165: New Line Productions Inc.; p. 166: Warner Bros. (Swank); Steve Granitz/Wireimage.com (Ryder); Lions Gate/Courtesy Everett Collection (Dafoe); p. 167: Focus Features/Courtesy Everett Collection (Carrey); Bettmann/Corbis (Keats); Michael Nicholson/Corbis (Wordsworth; Pope); Bettmann/Corbis (Byron); p. 168: Kelly A. Swift/Retna (Etheridge); Jeffrey Mayer/Wireimage.com (Nash) ; p. 169: 20th Century Fox/Courtesy Everett Collection (Crowe); Gail Oskin/Wireimage.com (Clinton); Steven Sands/Corbis Sygma (Barrymore); Bill Nation/Corbis Sygma (Shipp); Chris Walter/Wireimage.com (LL Cool J); p. 170: Terry Chostner/Lucasfilm Ltd./Photofest; p. 171: Artisan Entertainment/Courtesy Everett Collection (Requiem for a Dream); DreamWorks/Courtesy Everett Collection (Almost Famous); Paramount/Courtesy Everett Collection (Vanilla Sky); 20th Century Fox/Courtesy Everett Collection (Minority Report); p. 172: CBS/Courtesy Everett Collection (CSI); Helle Aasand/The Mississippi Press-Register/AP ('N Sync); ABC/Courtesy Everett Collection (Cross); p. 173: Francois Duhamel/20th Century Fox /DreamWorks/The Kobal Collection (Cast Away); Ryan McVay/Getty Images (ice skate); Siede Preis/Getty Images (bow); Stockdisc/Getty Images (golf club); p. 174: Jeffrey Mayer/Wireimage.com (Duff); James Devaney/Wireimage.com (Lohan); p. 175: HBO/Courtesy Everett Collection (Griffiths); Courtesy Sophie Giraud/IFC Films (My Big Fat Greek Wedding); DreamWorks/Courtesy Everett Collection (The Ring); 20th Century Fox/Courtesy Everett Collection (Joe Millionaire)